Hang Gliding

Pelham Books

Hang Gliding

Martin Hunt and David Hunn

with a section by **Dan Poynter**

Hang gliding, one pilot remarked, is not an experience you can really relate to someone who has not had it. This book is an attempt to prove him wrong.

First published 1977

© Martin Hunt 1977

ISBN: 0 7207 0975 X

This is an **Alphabook**
Designed and produced by Alphabet and Image, Sherborne, Dorset
Filmset and printed by BAS Printers Limited, Over Wallop, Hampshire

Contents

Can you never get enough? Eric Woods flies
VC 10s for a living, hang glides for pleasure.

.1 The Man

There are probably only three areas in the world where there are more hang gliders than there is room to fly them: parts of southern California; the hinterland of Sydney, New South Wales; and almost anywhere in south-east England. Find there a smooth and grassy hill facing the wind, a hill near the peak of which a car may be driven, and you will find the fraternity.

Unless you get up extraordinarily early, you will not have to reach the hill to be sure they are there. From a mile away something in the sky will catch your eye. Catch it and hold it, wondering, entranced: there, hanging in the air, is a great bird. There is another, swooping; and another, soaring. Their wings do not flap, no cry comes from the hidden throat. Do not drive on, yet, or you may end in a ditch—it takes a mighty will to resist this sight and concentrate on tarmac and the internal combustion engine.

When you have had your fill from that distance, keep your head down and concentrate. Draw nearer to the beautiful beasts, to the pterodactyls of today, and at the next stop the colours of their wings will ensnare you. Glorious, striped, patched, translucent, they wheel and dip, each holding a specimen of *Homo sapiens*. Some are sitting, like a child on a swing seat, some lying like a man in a hammock, but face down. Prisoners of the air, yet free men in it, they ride the invisible currents as though the hundred feet between you were the distance between heaven and earth. They may be right.

Up by the take-off ground, hang gliders are spread over the grass like butterflies on baize, tip to tip, nose to heel, so closely arrayed that the spectator's steps must be carefully picked. There one comes in, more like a reptile clutching his prey than you would believe. The great wings are tipped up by now, the creature stalls, and the legs of the captive hang and wriggle as he dangles in his harness, a living undercarriage ready for touchdown.

Here, one prepares to step into space: a friend or two steady the extremities and run with him as the pilot, bearing the weight over his head at the angle necessary for take-off, steps briskly into the task. He trots at the wind, kicks and is gone from the earth. Hesitant for a moment as if unsure of its readiness

for the journey, the wings waver almost within our reach. Immediately, the pilot pulls the nose down and they swoop, parallel to the steep slope, in silent acceleration. Now he has lifting speed. The nose eases back again and nature's huge, kind hand is under him. Up and away they go, into their world, out of ours.

'I first saw it on a television commercial,' one pilot says. 'I said straight away, that's for me.' Though you may yourself feel chicken about the prospect of being suspended so nakedly, defenceless in the middle of nothing, or nothing that you can see, it is hard not to share his enthusiasm. If God had meant us to fly, He would have given us wings? If He had meant us to stay on the ground, would He not perhaps have given us roots?

'I can only tell you,' says another, 'that there's nothing quite like it. Nothing.' There is a longish pause, as he downs a little beer, drags smoke through his minced tobacco, and reaches deep into his untidy mind. 'Sex is the nearest, but this lasts longer. Once you've done it, you can hardly wait till you can do it again.'

You cannot conveniently categorize hang-gliding people. By and large, they are what psychologists would call divergent thinkers—men and women of determination and independent spirit, nonconformists in the broadest sense. Many are self-employed, which confirms that character assessment as well as enabling them to spend more time hang gliding. As a species, they do

Lining up for take-off

Prototypes abound. Here a Hi-way Boomerang with truncated wing tips is test piloted to check its stability.

not drop into a mould, and have no intention of doing so. You will not find them toeing any line without good reason. As the organization of the sport becomes necessarily more secure and more regular, it meets more opposition from those who desire neither security nor regularity.

'I know we have to have an organization and we have to have rules, especially for safety,' admitted one enthusiast, 'but I liked the freedom of the early days. It was better then.' Back in 1973, when there were barely a hundred hang-glider fliers in Britain, one of them noted that the sport was free of 'red tape' because, unlike many leisure activities, 'we create no noise, discharge no pollutant and (hopefully) cause no damage.' Those are the virtues that make hang gliding a socially acceptable sport. 'But by the time we are a thousand strong, officialdom may well have cast a pragmatic eye in our direction. I rather suspect that, to the official mind, a whole group of people being allowed to flit merrily about the sky unchecked borders on insurgency.'

The controls exercised by the British Hang Gliding Association have at least served the excellent purpose of impressing the authorities. Though these insurgents are now more than three thousand strong, they still do not need a licence for take-off. Long may it be so, and as we spectators gasp in admiration at the beauty of the sight above us, let us do our bit to keep them free, wherever in the world we are, by not being a nuisance: by parking off the road, but not in a farmer's field; by shutting farmers' gates and taking our litter with us; by keeping dogs away from the immediate flying scene (landing a hang glider is a tricky enough business without having to do it down the throat of a hound who looks as if what he wants most in the world is hang-gliding trousers, shortly followed by hang-gliding buttocks). That is the first and last sermon you will find in this book.

2 The Machine

Everybody knows what a hang glider is. One of those pretty, coloured kites that people hang on to and jump off hill tops and glide down to the bottom. But *exactly* what is a hang glider? This definition was approved at the inaugural meeting of the International Hang Gliding Commission in June, 1975:

> A hang glider is a heavier-than-air, fixed-wing (i.e. not rotating-wing) glider, which is capable of being carried, foot-launched and landed solely by the energy and use of the pilot's legs.

That says little, but enough. It does not, note, include any restriction on shape or size—as long as the machine is 'capable of being carried'. Some hang gliders have the form, in miniature, of conventional gliding monoplanes. There is not much body to them, but there is a small tailplane and the wings are of rigid or semi-rigid material. Some of these have adjustable flaps at the trailing edges, connected by cables to a control stick. The tendency today is, however, for these gliders to become less rigid and for their wings to sweep back more, thus drawing them closer to the vast majority of the hang gliders of the world—simple, delta-shaped wings under which the pilot hangs in a harness. The wing fabric is not rigid, and the craft is so designed that it can easily and quickly be folded up and stowed in a tubular bag.

Hang gliders of this type all derive from the principle established in the late 1940s by an American scientist, Dr Francis Rogallo, and as a species have taken his name. Though the finer points of the design of each one embody the sophisticated use of aerodynamics, the skeleton is simplicity indeed. A Rogallo-type hang glider is likely to consist of four aluminium alloy tubes, between one and two inches in diameter. Three of them form an arrowhead—one the central keel, the others the swept-back leading edges of each wing. The fourth is the crosstube, which may be about eighteen feet long. It crosses the keel, to which it is joined, at right angles, and joins the leading edge tubes, usually about two-thirds of the way from front to back.

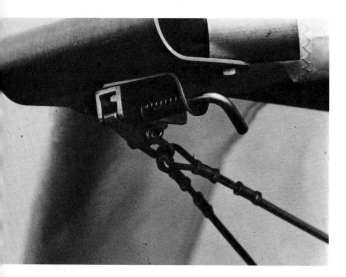

On landing, the pilot uses a spring-loaded catch shown above to release the front flying wires. This allows the glider to lie flat on the ground ready for folding, as shown below. At the very heart of things is the *Jesus bolt, right,* where the crosstube is joined to the triangular control frame. Most of the rigging wires run down to the lower corners of this frame, as shown below right and in the flight picture opposite.

That concludes the basic framework—a wide 'A' lying on a central keel, light, but tough enough to take knocks. Each tube junction is held fast by a bolt, several of which can be quickly released and reassembled, to facilitate the frequent rigging and derigging procedures.

The fabric of the wings must be tough, non-porous and stretch-resistant, again without being too heavy—with a leading edge of 18 feet, some 240 square feet of sail are involved—but the total weight of the machine is kept down to about 40 lb (18 kilograms). Ripstop nylon similar to that used in parachutes used to be popular, but in much of the world today terylene (dacron) sailcloth has become the proved and standard material. It is sewn over the leading edge tubes and the keel tube, but not over the crosstube, so that in flight the sails are inflated in two splendid billows.

Beneath the point at which the crosstube passes under the keel, the pilot and his control frame are suspended. The frame is an aluminium vertical triangle, its apex bolted to the junction by what is known reasonably as the heart bolt and irreverently as the Jesus bolt. (Before the question has left his lips, the inquirer realises the answer: it is the heart of the hang glider, and 'Jesus!' is what the pilot may well exclaim if the bolt fails.) The apex is not pointed, but flat for just sufficient width to provide a secure union with the crosstube. Near the base of this triangular frame, a few inches up from each corner, steel rigging cable runs to each end of the keel and each end of the crosstube, locking the control frame to the main structure. The pilot's harness is of such a length that, by pushing against the control frame, he can shift his body weight from one side to another, affecting the attitude of the hang glider as he does so.

Above the wing, there is more rigging cable. On most hang gliders, a short length of tubing called the king post sticks vertically up above the sail from

the keel and crosstube junction, and from its head cables run, again to the four extremities of the craft. This gives added strength to the whole airframe, and the post itself provides a useful fender to protect the sails from damage when the glider is turned upside down—whether deliberately or accidentally.

In early Rogallo designs, the pilot was merely suspended in a parachute harness, which is not the most comfortable way to fly. Into this was later incorporated a small seat, so positioned that in flight the bottom bar of the control frame is at chest height to the seated pilot. For take-off and landing, the pilot slips off the seat, so that although he is still harnessed, his legs are free. (Larger machines can be adapted to take a pilot and passenger, side by side, a useful instructional ploy.) More recently, many pilots have come to prefer the prone flying position, in which more effective control can be exercised and the body, though in an unnatural posture, presents much less resistance to air flow.

A sling supports the body from shoulders to knees, at such a level that the head and shoulders are within the triangle. The feet may rest in stirrups. These slings are so hung that the pilot can, with the minimum effort, reach the prone position as soon as he has taken off, and leave it in time for landing in the usual way. Whether or not the prone position is safer than the upright one in case of crashes is a point about which there is some doubt. It is generally agreed that prone fliers are less likely to be injured in minor accidents, as the first impact on landing is taken by the control frame instead of the pilot's legs; but in crashes of greater violence, the uncomfortable truth must be faced that the part of the body most likely to hit something is the head.

And so to helmets. Despite the highly independent attitudes of most hang-glider pilots, who as a breed resent restrictions and regulations, all but the really wild men agree that anyone who goes up without a crash hat barely deserves to survive. The British Hang Gliding Association has achieved a remarkable success rate in this matter by its policy of persuasion rather than regulation. Beyond the helmet, clothes tend to be chosen for comfort rather than safety. Good strong boots are recommended, not only for their ability to absorb shock, but for their usefulness in climbing up the hill again; gloves protect the knuckles from abrasion, but do an even more important job by keeping the hands warm. It can be very cold up there, particularly when you are hanging on to a metal bar, and once the pilot acquires numb fingers, he has lost maximum control. Americans, with their background of armoured football costume, tend to wear knee and elbow pads more than others do. What matters most, after the helmet and boots, is that the flier should dress for the weather. This is likely to mean overalls and thick woollens in the winter, overalls and nothing much in the summer.

Flight suit, harness for prone flying, helmet. Inside it all is Johnny Carr.

*Two standard Rogallo models : a single and,
above, a dual with 'West Country' sail cut.*

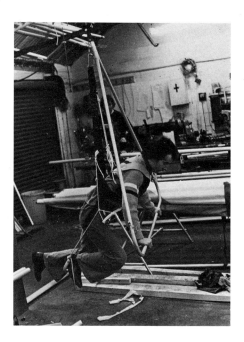

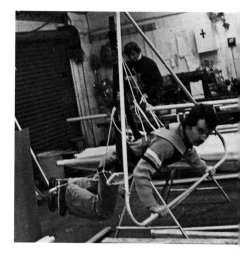

*You need to climb into a
prone harness swiftly and
smoothly. Practising in the
workshop will help the pilot
to avoid getting tangled with
the stirrups when in the air.*

With that fixed as your picture of the average, universal hang glider and pilot, we can look a little more deeply into the individuality of the man and his machine. Some, as we have said, are big enough to carry two. There are in fact three classes of hang glider internationally accepted: Class 1, standard Rogallo, with control only by weight shifting; Class 2, open class, maximum 40 kilograms (90 lb) empty, including instruments; Class 3, unrestricted, maximum weight 50 kilograms (110 lb), including instruments. Some hang gliders are specially built to withstand the stress of being tow-lifted on water by a motor boat. Some, as we shall learn later, carry their own motor-propulsion for assisting take-off. Though pressure and persuasion have largely eliminated the practice, it used to be common to assemble hang gliders from kits, or even to build your own to a plan. The determination, in well-organized hang-gliding nations, to raise the standards of safety and reliability has led to nearly all craft now being bought ready-made and fully-assembled.

Though the Rogallo concept predominates, it is not exclusive. The limitations imposed on the designer are those of his personal dream of hang gliding. The fact that the official definition requires the machine to be light enough to carry and to launch single-handed is of little consequence. What matters is that this is the way the enthusiast wants it. He wants to be able to shove his glider in a bag and strap it on the roof of his car, unpack and rig it in a few minutes and take off without formality (but with, always, the presence

The prone harness helps to stream-line the pilot's body in flight.

Left and below: early non-Rogallo types, Miles Wing Gulp (GB) and Quicksilver (USA).

of at least one other adult, the minimum requirement for emergencies). He wants to be able to derig at the bottom of the hill and lug it up to the top again; not wait for someone to arrive with a truck to collect him. He wants to sling the package under his garage roof when he gets home, not to occupy the whole garage with it.

It is these desires for independence and simplicity that have led designers away from conventional aircraft configurations, and caused most of them to abandon, for instance, the use of a tailplane. This would certainly give finer control, but complicates every other step of a hang-glider owner's life. As you could see from the introduction to this book, most of them just want to be like birds. When that is said, however, there remains a good deal of scope for diversity and foible—as much as there is between the albatross and the eagle, the swallow and the swift. Even within the general layout of a Rogallo, two hang gliders can have vitally differing characteristics, both visual and

Pilots fly prone, seated or, right, supine—unusual but clearly the most comfortable for long flights.

aerodynamic, and the many different designers and manufacturers of the craft see to it that their own creations are instantly recognizable.

Think of a Rogallo lying flat on the ground below you, a simple triangle. By changing the relative lengths of the keel and the leading edges, and by altering the angle of the nose, the whole shape of the machine changes. It may be a streamlined arrow or a broad one. It could have, and often does, its wing tips snipped off or the trailing edge of the sail scalloped in a variety of shapes; and the sail area will have been carefully chosen by the buyer as the one best suited to his body weight (the available range runs at least from 120 to 280

Two Rogallos may be no more alike than two Fords. One may have a curved boom (top left), another a curved keel (lower right). Sails may be cut Chevron (top right) or Sunburst (lower left).

square feet). See the hang glider from the side, and the keel itself may be curved up or down. See it flying towards you, and you will see that the wing tips may be higher than the keel or lower, effected by the curve or angle of the crosstube.

To the eyes of those who remain on the ground, nothing is more memorable than the sail fabric itself, so gloriously cut and coloured. If you examined it, you would find that the sail is sewn together from several panels of material, which can be of almost any shape and colour, and which determine, at the designer's will, the amount of billow in the inflated sail; the amount and its precise position. Pockets similar to those sewn into the fabric

Top left, Australian, and top right American Sunbird Strato have scalloped trailing edges. Lower left is a Dragonfly with truncated tips and window panels; the Cobra, lower right, has trailing edge battens and unusual tail form.

to enable it to be fitted to the airframe may also be provided to accommodate battens that vary the stiffness of the final form, and may even be used to trap air and vary the aerofoil shape in flight.

All these refinements affect the flight character of the machine in ways that need not concern the spectator, for whom they provide an infinite variety of charm and fascination. Happily, the sailcloth is translucent, allowing the intensity and direction of the day's light to play pretty tricks with the colours; and allowing the owner to weave his own visual magic with inks and dyes. Not only for the graceful poetry of its motion is hang gliding paramount among the world's most beautiful sports.

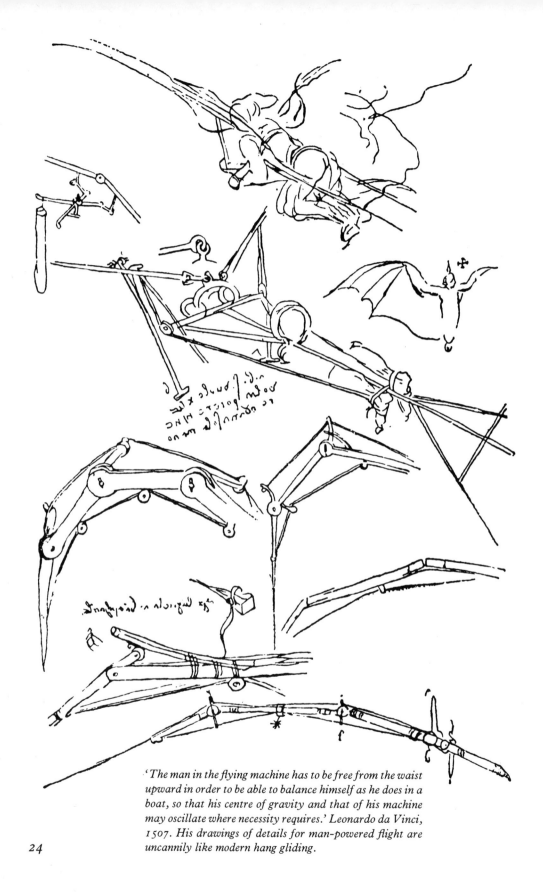

'The man in the flying machine has to be free from the waist upward in order to be able to balance himself as he does in a boat, so that his centre of gravity and that of his machine may oscillate where necessity requires.' Leonardo da Vinci, 1507. His drawings of details for man-powered flight are uncannily like modern hang gliding.

3 The Story

From Daedalus and da Vinci to Lilienthal and Rogallo, the story of man's attempts to fly free as a bird is an absurd mixture of heroism and farce, triumph and tragedy. Even now, towards the end of the twentieth century, men still fasten wings to their arms and flap frantically, to drop year by year into the sea during the Selsey Birdman Rally, in England. There is still a magical attraction about the thought of floating on air, not cocooned in a jet-propelled tube, but open and unhampered, your face to the airflow. That is the secret of the true hang glider's success: the single, simple, delta-shaped wing does not attempt to defeat nature, but to use and understand it. It tries to put the pilot on a par with the birds.

According to Greek legend, that is all Daedalus did. He may have been inspired, as many of his successors were, by nature's own hang-gliding miracle, the *Pteranodon ingens*. This prehistoric reptile was the largest flying creature known to exist. Palaeontologists believe it weighed only 35 pounds, but may have had had a wingspan of 54 feet; this must have made it a poor example of powered flight, but a very efficient glider, with an extremely low sink rate and low flying and stalling speed. They also believe it may have nested on cliffs facing the sea and the prevailing wind, returning home by soaring up the cliff face and flopping down gently on the top.

Returning was not a problem that arose in the case of Daedalus. The builder of the labyrinth for Minos, in which the great king's wife is said to have had intercourse with a bull and given birth to a minotaur, he was himself imprisoned in it. There was no way out except by air, and Daedalus and his son got down to the job with feathers, needle and thread, and wax. It worked a treat for papa, who took off like a dream and flew, with only one touchdown, all the way from Crete to Greece. But young Icarus, his son, did not listen to the old man's lecture in basic aerodynamics: do not fly too low, or the sea spray will wet your feathers; nor too high, or the sun will melt the wax. Boys will be boys: Icarus obviously soared to phenomenal heights, from which he took an early bath and was buried on the island that came to be called Icaria.

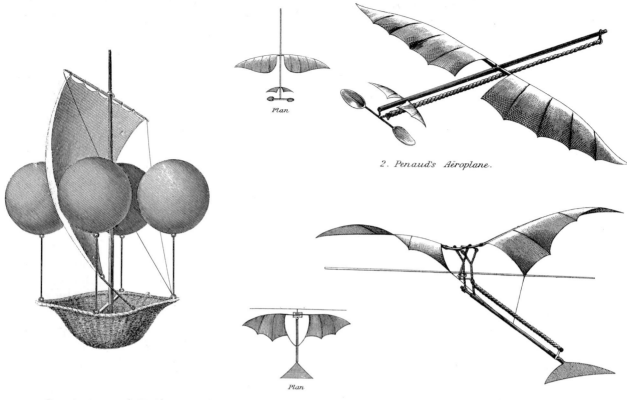

Lanas Aeronautic Machine

2. *Penaud's Aëroplane.*

Plan

3. *Penaud's Mechanical Bird.*

Leonardo da Vinci, the fifteenth-century Italian genius whose scientific talents took him from the double lavatory seat to the dynamics of fluids, designed something that looked remarkably like a hang glider. It was his imaginative exercise that fired a succession of medieval nutters into leaping from tower tops. Many, apparently, were of clerical bent and believed that with wings, man was nearer to the angels, and thus to God. With a ninety-degree glide angle, they no doubt reached their Maker swiftly.

One distinguished man of the church, Bishop Wilkins of Chester, was not fool enough to try it, but foresaw in the seventeenth century that the challenge would one day be met: 'If fowl can so easily move itself up and down in the air without so much as stirring the wings, it is not improbable that when men by long practice have arrived to any skill and experience, they will come very near unto the imitation of Nature.' What distinguished that forecast was the Bishop's abandonment of the flapping process and his extraordinary perception of the process of soaring, which 400 years later is the goal of most hang-glider pilots.

At about the same time, a Jesuit monk, Francisco de Lana, began contemplating lighter-than-air flight. What was needed, he reasoned rightly, was a container full of something that weighed less than air. Nothing then known fulfilled the need—except no air at all. He designed a man-carrying airship supported by four balloons of thin copper, each containing a vacuum.

The eighteenth-century origins of today's balloons—a hot air 'Montgolfière' left, and the 'Charlière', above, that rose 2000 feet on smokeless fuel, hydrogen.

Had the craft been constructed, it is unlikely to have lasted long since the atmospheric pressure would have caused the copper containers to collapse. However, de Lana abandoned the idea without practice, believing that any attempt to fly would be interpreted by his Creator as impiety.

He clearly had his finger on a sound principle, and ballooning began to interest more inventors. A French priest, Galien, had the impractical idea of filling a bag with low-density air from higher altitudes, but it was the isolation of hydrogen by Henry Cavendish in 1766 that opened the door to success. At the same time that experiments were continuing on that field, the French paper-making brothers, Etienne and Joseph Montgolfièr, discovered idly that, just as smoke from a fire rises in the air, a paper bag full of smoke also rises. They thought this a special property of smoke, calling it levity.

Though their scientific analysis was incorrect, they proved the principle to be sound when, in November 1783, they sent two compatriots successfully aloft on a five-mile trip, filling the balloon with smoke from a fire of wool and straw. Just ten days later Professor J. A. Charles rose 2,000 feet with no smoke and no fire, in a hydrogen balloon. Hot air ballooning in 'Montgolfières' (the principle is that air, whether smoky or not, expands when heated. Less is needed to fill a balloon so the balloon is lighter) was abandoned in favour of 'Charlières', and hydrogen remained the stable lighter-than-air gas until the airship Hindenberg was destroyed by fire in 1937.

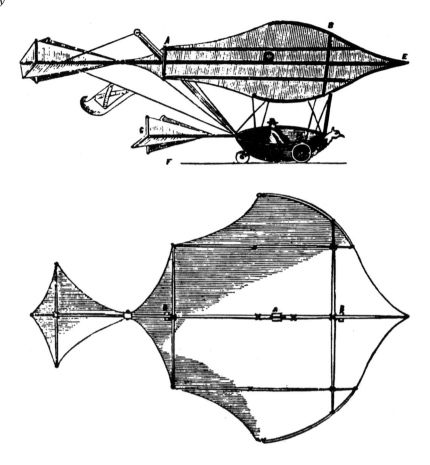

In the year when men first rose in balloons, a boy in Scarborough, England, had his tenth birthday. His achievements in flight were to be sensational—he was the true inventor of the aeroplane—though nothing was more shattering than the fact that they were not recognized for nearly a century. Sir George Cayley's ideas were so far ahead of his time that they were almost totally ignored, and even now in his own country his name means nothing beside that of the Wright brothers. But Cayley successfully built and flew several pilotless gliders of remarkably advanced design in the first half of the nineteenth century, at least one of which was depicted in his sketch book with a man lying along the keel. If this idea was ever put into effect (no evidence has been found), it would have anticipated Lilienthal by 75 years.

Cayley subsequently designed many gliders of man-carrying potential, in one of which he instructed his coachman to make a flight. It was modestly successful, launched by the muscle power of the villagers running downhill pulling ropes, but on landing the coachman is said to have left the squire's employment immediately, unwilling to be subjected to such unnatural

Shown left is one of the plans of the brilliant and largely unrecognised early eighteenth century pioneer, Sir George Cayley. Put into practice 120 years later for television, it actually flew.

processes again. In 1972 a British television company, Anglia, asked Commander John Sproule to recreate this flight. Sproule chose for the job a machine outlined in detail in the *Mechanics Magazine* of September 1852, 'Sir George Cayley's Governable Parachute'. The mainsail and tailplane were, in plan, not unlike the shape of a giant ray fish, with a length of forty feet and a sail area of 460 square feet.

Suspended below the sail was a three-wheeled wooden carriage of broad canoe shape, from which a long spar controlled a rudder, separate from and below the tailplane. Sproule's replica, a magnificent machine, took to the air briefly under human launch (it was much heavier than Cayley's original specification of 160 lb), and superbly under the influence of a towing car. It rose to thirty feet and flew across the dale beside which Cayley used to live until, in Sproule's words, 'the nose dropped, there was a loud bang and the front axle broke, and the tail fell off.' Nevertheless it landed without disaster.

Cayley had died content in 1857, and it was nearly thirty years before the next significant advance was made in getting man airborne. In 1883 John J.

The unbelievable flying whatnot of Clement Ader, who in 1890 persuaded his steam-propelled creation to leave the ground.

Montgomery was able to control the flight of his glider from a hilltop near San Diego, California; in 1890 Clément Ader persuaded a steam-propelled monoplane into the air for about fifty yards; and shortly after that the historic work emerged of Otto Lilienthal, the greatest figure of unpowered flight.

Lilienthal was born in Anklam, Germany, in 1848. After some early experiments with ornithopters ('bird machines'), he turned to gliding and built many efficient and most beautiful gliders of bird-like appearance and sound aerodynamic construction, from which he hung by the armpits. Nothing conveys the excitement and intelligence of his work better than Lilienthal's own words:

> From a raised starting point, particularly from the top of a flat hill, one can, after some practice, soar through the air, reaching the earth only after having gone a great distance. For this purpose I have hitherto employed a sailing apparatus very like the outspread pinions of a soaring bird. It consists of a wooden frame covered with shirting (cotton twill). The frame is supporting the body. The legs remain free for running and jumping. The steering in the air is brought about by changing the centre of gravity.

*Otto Lilienthal,
the birdman*

This apparatus I had constructed with supporting surfaces of ten to twenty square metres. The larger sailing surfaces move in an incline of one to eight, so that one is enabled to fly eight times as far as the starting hill is high. The steering is facilitated by the rudder, which is firmly fastened behind in a horizontal and vertical position. The machines weigh, according to their size, from fifteen to twenty kilograms (33 to 55 pounds). In order to practise flying with these sailing surfaces [the pilot] first takes short jumps on a somewhat inclined surface till he has accustomed himself to be borne by the air. Finally he is able to sail over inclined surfaces as far as he wishes. The supporting capacity of the air is felt, particularly if there is a breeze. A sudden increase in the wind causes a longer stoppage in the air, or one is raised to a still higher point. The charm of such flight is indescribable, and there could not be a healthier motion or more exciting sport in the open air.

The apparatus which I now employ in my flying exercises contains a great many improvements as compared with the first sailing surfaces with which I commenced this kind of experiment five years ago. The first attempts in windy weather taught me that suitable steering surfaces would be needed to enable me to keep my course better against the wind. Repeated changes in the construction led to a kind of apparatus with which [the pilot] can throw himself without danger from any height, reaching the earth safely after a long distance. The construction of the machine is such that it resembles in all its parts a strut frame, the joints of which are calculated to stand pull and pressure in order to combine the greatest strength with the least weight.

An important improvement was to arrange the apparatus for folding. All of my recent machines are so arranged that they can be taken through a door two metres high. The unfolding and putting together of

Lilienthal: 'From a raised starting point one can, after some practice, soar through the air, reaching earth only after having gone a great distance.'

the flying implements takes about two minutes. A single grip of the hands is sufficient to attach the apparatus safely to the body, and one gets out of the apparatus just as quickly on landing. In case of storm, the flying sail is folded up in half a minute and can be laid by anywhere. If one should not care to fold the apparatus, [one] may await the end of the storm under cover of the wings, which are capable of protecting twenty persons.

Between 1893 and his death in 1896, Lilienthal made more than 2,000 flights, most of them from a fifty-foot artificial hill near his home outside Berlin. To a degree never before realised, he was able to harness the airflow to provide lift and maintain flight. He was even occasionally able to soar, and once made a flight that covered more than 1,000 feet.

If the atmosphere is undisturbed, the experimenter sails with uniform speed; as soon, however, as even a slight breeze springs up, the course of the flight becomes irregular. The apparatus inclines now to the right, now to the left. The person flying ascends from the usual line of flight, and borne by the wind, suddenly remains floating at a point high in the air; the onlookers hold their breath; all at once cheers are heard, the sailer proceeds and glides amid the joyful exclamations of the multitude in a graceful curve back again to earth.

Can any sport be more exciting than flying? Strength and adroitness, courage and decision, can nowhere gain such triumphs as in these gigantic bounds into the air when the gymnast safely steers his soaring machine house-high over the heads of the spectators. That the danger here is easily avoided when one practises in a reasonable way, I have sufficiently proved, as I myself have made thousands of experiments within the last five years, and have had no accidents whatever, a few scratches excepted. But all this is only a means to the end; our aim remains to develop human flight to as high a standard as possible.

He had always worked on the same principle of control by weight shifting that Rogallo hang gliders use today. It was when he was experimenting with a movable elevator that a sudden gust of wind caused his glider to go into a spin. He dived to the ground from fifty feet, broke his spine and died a few hours later, aged 48.

A year before that tragedy a British contemporary, marine engineer Percy Pilcher, began his experiments with a similar type of glider, slightly larger and distinguished by the phenomenal number of rigging wires that held it stable. Both men hung below the wings, but Pilcher often used a tow-launch. Both men died on the threshold of powered flight, and both intended to use the power not as an end in itself, but to take them up to heights at which they could glide better. Pilcher had his engine ready to use and, in bad weather, was demonstrating his glider to Lord Braye at Market Harborough, Northamptonshire, when he crashed and was fatally injured.

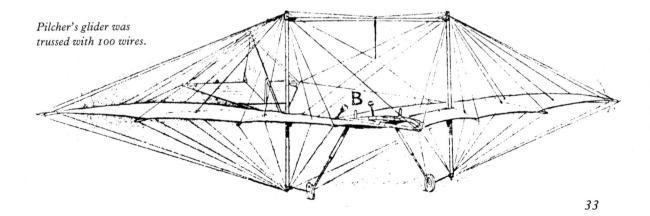

Pilcher's glider was trussed with 100 wires.

Octave Chanute, 'father of the modern biplane'.

It was a very small step from Lilienthal/Pilcher to the Wrights, but the step did exist in the remarkable human form of Octave Chanute—'the father of the modern biplane'. French-born and American-bred, he began gliding when he was more than sixty years old, in the year Lilienthal died. On the shores of Lake Michigan, near Chicago, he and his group of experimenters made more than 1,000 flights. He wrote the book *Progress in Flying Machines* that became the basic text for the Wrights, with whom he had a close relationship.

Those history-making American brothers did not, as is sometimes popularly suggested, accidentally discover the secret of powered flight while working in their bicycle shop. They began tests on kites in 1899, moving on through tethered gliders and free-flight gliders to man-carrying jobs that they flew on the sand dunes of Kitty Hawk, in North Carolina's constant and predictable winds. Their first man-carrying glider had a span of seventeen feet and wing elevators; in a 27-foot span glider, in 1901, they achieved a glide of 300 feet; and in 1902 they had a front-mounted rudder as well as an elevator on their biplane. On the morning of 17 December, 1903, Orville Wright took off under power—a 16 horse power, chain-driven, petrol engine with two rear-mounted propellors—and maintained flight for a period that historians estimate variously as between twelve and sixty seconds. His airspeed reached beyond 30 mph though the ground speed was only 8 mph. There are those who believe it a pity that Wright's search for perfection in pure flight should have come to such an impure conclusion.

It is doubtful whether history will ever deny Wright his achievement, but it is fair to say that there have subsequently emerged other, less well-authenticated candidates for the honour of having made the first powered flight of appreciable size. A New Zealand farmer, Richard Pearse, is said to have made several flights at tree-top level at least a year before Wright, and on 31 March, 1903, he made two-and-a-half circuits of a small field before twenty-five witnesses.

A Texan railway ticket agent, according to some sources, beat the Wright flight by six years between two villages in McLennan County, but the most intriguing of these supposedly historic flights was reputedly made by a German school-teacher, Jacob Brodbeck, who also lived in Texas. He had spent much of his spare time in Germany trying to make for the Kaiser a spring-powered clock that would run for ever without winding, and in Texas he applied similar principles to aero engine power. The idea was that the pilot would continue to rewind one end of the spring while the other drove the propellor. His plane, it is said, did take off near San Antonio in 1865. It made sufficient height for its fall to destroy the aircraft completely, though Brodbeck escaped serious injury.

From the moment of the Wrights' acclaimed triumph, the efforts of the aeronautically-inclined world were directed towards powered flight, which by the time of the First World War had taken man across the English Channel (Bleriot, 1909) and soon afterwards took men non-stop across the Atlantic (Alcock and Brown, 1919). It was at this point, paradoxically, that the arts of gliding began once more to be fully explored. The Treaty of Versailles imposed strict limitations on the building and use of powered aircraft in Germany, and it was here, in Lilienthal's land, that gliding became established as a sport.

Though hang gliding as such made little significant advance throughout the first half of the twentieth century, there was one achievement that should be recorded. Rheinhold Platz, the Fokker designer, built a most beautiful job known as the Platz Sailwing, controlled on the principle of sloop-rigged sailing boats. The pilot sat on the keel, in front of the immobile 'mainsail', and steered the craft by operating one or other, or both, of the 'jib sails' in front of him. Less a hang glider than an air yacht, it remains, so far as we know, a unique specimen—and it flew.

Wilbur Wright at the controls of the gliding biplane. The Wright Brothers used gliders to get to power.

4 Staying Up

Every flight is like a dream—one that you have planned, but still takes you by surprise, sweeps you unexpectedly away, thrusts decisions at you for which you are not prepared. In one second you are carrying the beautiful beast, in the next the dominance has switched and it is you that is borne. First the strength and drive is yours, as you hold the vast bird above your head, accurately angled, perfectly directed: one, two, three, four—you pump your feet into the turf and with every step the wind you face lifts a little of the burden from your arms. Five, six, seven—you are weightless now. A kick and you have gone.

Now you are the inanimate object, held and for an instant helpless; the life and power of the partnership has passed to the wing above you. It pulls you abruptly off the hill, dangles you over its rapidly-receding slope, and in that brief moment of shocked exhilaration you are a prisoner. No time for dreams now: the nose must come down before the wind takes you too far, the mastery must be yours. Give it speed, give it glide, order it to obey.

Settle now in quiet command, delicately adjusting, finely judging the angle of attack that will take you across the hill and over the warm thrust that should rise from the ploughed field that lies beyond it, a ruddy patch amid the gold and green. You edge into it, and nature's currents support you. Motionless first, you hover; then gently you soar up, just as the gulls are doing beside you. Like you, they turn a little, rock a little, but without effort, without wingbeat, they ride ever higher on the magic carpet that is your invisible elevator.

This is the bliss that dreams should be made of, this the long moment when reality is left behind. As you nose out of the thermal lift, high above the hard and noisy world you know too well, you are alone and supreme. What has earth-bound man ever experienced to equal this, to enable him even to understand it? You know what it is like to step out into the air at the top of the Eiffel Tower? In hang gliding you have done that—and kept on going. Only the steady flutter of the wing, and the grip of its harness, reminds you that

Rising on a thermal to the cumulus

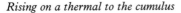

you do have, and need, that man-made ally above you, that you are not quite alone as you float on air.

You are high enough now to make a return journey. Gently out, into the wind, time to see and to savour the pattern of life below. Not the busy pulse of life, because even from up here there are only two roads in sight; away to the left a dark worm slinks into its hillside hole, and that is a train and a tunnel. Otherwise, life as hang-glider pilots see it is unbelievably peaceful. The smoke from two cottage chimneys is rudely dispersed by the breeze that made you airborne, the hedges stitch the fields together, the cows amble like farmyard toys. Stop the world, someone said, I want to get off. He must have got off here.

Mike Robinson hangs over the England-Wales border.

Time to turn now and head back to the landing site. Never take turns for granted, they punish you when you least expect it. A nice wide one here, not too much height lost, and you are on line for home. Now the wind is with you, and like an arrow you pierce the air. There is a certain wild joy about speeding up a motorway on a motorbike; here you treble it—no traffic, no road, no engine. Hard to believe that perfection can come any purer.

All too soon the hill top is at hand, busy as an ant hill, so strewn with the coloured leaves that are hang gliders at rest that for a moment you lose the landing spot. Push left to line it up, ease up the nose, this could be tricky.

Much too fast to make a landing with the wind, that is why you are told not to do it. Overshooting now, push the bar out. Too far too soon, your stall is too high. This could be a heavy bump. The lads below are scurrying—not out of the way, but just where you will need them. Thump with the boots, stagger, going over.

There is something specially humiliating about dragging your face across the grass, apart from the pain. 'Serves you right, you silly clown,' they say as they pick you up. It does, it did. You remember and you learn, but that is no guarantee against your trying it again. Always a dream, always a challenge.

One of this book's writers spent most of his life in puzzled but contented ignorance as to what magic it was that prevented ships from sinking. A

Undignified execution of ground loop calls for urgent friendly assistance.

similar defiance of nature enabled aeroplanes to lift him from Heathrow and deposit him gently on the runway at JFK, New York, and there did not seem any sense in it. Thus can a life be deranged simply by missing school on the day we were told how Archimedes had jumped out of his bath and rushed down the street crying 'Eureka!'

What he had discovered, if you will allow yourself to believe it, does explain a good deal. This Greek mathematician decided, twenty-two centuries ago, that when a body is placed in fluid, an upward thrust acts against it that is equal to the weight of the fluid the body is displacing. If the body is a light one, very little upward thrust will be needed to keep it afloat. Your plastic duck seems to sit on top of the bath water, because even the slight indentation it makes on the surface displaces enough water, perhaps just a spoonful, to equal in weight the ounce or so of the duck.

With a heavy little body, a stone, the upward thrust will not be enough to prevent it sinking, but it may sink surprisingly slowly. As Archimedes discovered, the stone weighs less in the water than out of it. Move on to ships in the sea, and the hull of the vessel will settle down until it has displaced the amount of water that weighs as much as the ship itself. Put a load of passengers on, and it will settle lower until the scales are level again.

So it begins to seem less unreasonable that a ship floats, and in one further step we are airborne: it only needs the acceptance that, like any gas, air may not be liquid, but it is fluid. Start at the easy end, with a toy balloon. Blow it up yourself, seal it and let go, and the balloon will very gently find its way to the floor. It is displacing, say, half a cubic foot of air; but inside is the same air, just as if your ship were full of water, and the weight of the skin is enough to make it drop to the ground.

But go to one of those fêtes where they pump the balloon full of hydrogen, which is fourteen times lighter than air, and up it goes out of sight. Apply this to rather more serious flight, and you soon reach airships, those weird affairs that barely made it as useful aircraft. Some of them displaced five million cubic feet of air, producing an upward thrust capable of supporting 200 tons of airship. The drawback was that the skin of the craft had to be so thin it was extremely vulnerable. Hydrogen is so inflammable that the fire risk proved intolerable; its replacement by helium, which is twice as heavy and much more expensive, reduced the potential lifting power of the airship so greatly, in terms of passengers and cargo, that the whole principle ceased to be viable for either commercial or military use—though Londoners had cause to bless that offspring, the barrage balloon, during the Second World War.

With that basic Archimedean principle established we have moved into aerodynamics, at least in so far as they concern lighter-than-air craft. There is the first of flying's four great forces: lift. And there, working directly against lift, is the second: weight, which so interested Sir Isaac Newton when the apple dropped on his head. Any body of any weight within the earth's atmosphere wants to get back to earth. It will only be prevented from doing so if its displacement of air generates sufficient lift to support it. An apple or a solid metal ball do not. Moreover, two metal balls of the same size dropped from the same height will reach the ground at the same time, even if one is made of lead and the other aluminium. Their downward acceleration is constant.

Despite that, it is obvious what the result will be if you drop your ball of lead and another of the same weight, but vastly bigger, made of plastic foam. If you could watch the beginning of the drop in detail, you would see that they start by accelerating at the same speed, but the plastic one soon stops accelerating and reaches a constant speed. Another force is working on it: one that acts against the direction of travel and is called drag. A ball thrown across

Good coastal ridge lift draws all sorts to Torrey Pines, California.

a field meets it (that is one reason why you cannot throw a football as far as a cricket ball); a balloon rising into the sky meets it; a man jumping out of an aeroplane meets it. His body goes on accelerating until the drag force acting against him (which increases with speed) equals the weight force that is pulling him down. From then on, his speed of fall remains constant, at about 120 mph, until his parachute opens. The size and shape of the canopy sharply increase the drag at that speed, and the body's fall slows until once again the weight and drag forces are equal, which occurs at a speed of about 15 mph.

Lift, weight and drag: the three natural forces that act on all aircraft, lighter or heavier-than-air. Flying's fourth force is the one man designed to override all others: thrust. All powered aircraft—aeroplanes, airships or rockets—produce thrust by the operation of engines within a strength and direction range determined by the designer and selected by the pilot according to the needs of the moment. Thrust is what mostly takes one from Cape Kennedy to the moon, or from London to New York. Apart from a small amount of human thrust in take-off, hang gliders get by without it. But of the three natural forces already examined, one does not seem relevant to heavier-than-air machines: lift. Even without a body aboard, a hang glider, like a Boeing 747, is heavier than air. Chuck it off the roof top on a still day, and it will come down to rest in the garden—though not necessarily yours. Clip yourself in its harness and stand in a field, and no natural forces short of a gale will cause you to rise in the air. The amount of air displaced by you and your glider together does not equal your own body weight. So where does the lift come from?

On now to the second step of aerodynamics—and back, for a moment, to water. To understand the way in which man, by the art of his design, can persuade nature to lift his heavy craft into the air, you should take a ride in a rowing boat, but let somebody else pull the oars. Hold a short piece of thin board horizontally in the water, edge on to the flow. Hold it by an end, and you will feel that although it cuts easily enough through the water (as long as your oarsman is putting his back into the job), there is a slight force working on it (drag) that is trying to pull it out of your hand. Now angle the front edge up slightly, by about 15 degrees. You will have to hold tight, because not only is the drag increasing as a greater surface area meets the water, but there is also a positive force trying to lift the board out of the water. Lift is the word: think of the board as an aeroplane wing and the water as the air flowing against it. Twist the board further and you will soon find that eddies begin to form at the back edge. As they do, the lifting force decreases and the drag gets much stronger: your wing is stalling.

Before moving into the subtleties of aerofoil design, it is worth while staying with your board in the water (or, if you like, a piece of cardboard held similarly through the air) to analyse the precise direction of the forces acting

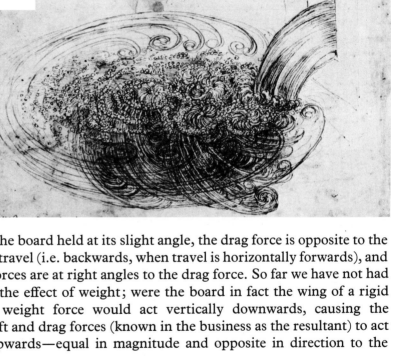

on it. With the board held at its slight angle, the drag force is opposite to the direction of travel (i.e. backwards, when travel is horizontally forwards), and the lifting forces are at right angles to the drag force. So far we have not had to consider the effect of weight; were the board in fact the wing of a rigid glider, the weight force would act vertically downwards, causing the combined lift and drag forces (known in the business as the resultant) to act vertically upwards—equal in magnitude and opposite in direction to the weight.

All unpowered heavier-than-air machines can only maintain flight by employing an efficient flying surface, one designed to produce lift. In effect this aerofoil, as the wing is called, is never flat. In section, its upper surface is always curved—not regularly, like an inverted saucer, but with the highest point of the curve occurring about a quarter of the way back from the leading (front) edge. From that apex, the upper surface of the aerofoil tapers gently

back till it meets the underside at the trailing edge (back). To understand the reason for this is absolutely vital to the understanding of flight. Back to water.

Imagine a canal down which a constant amount of water flows. For a few yards, where it is carried in an aqueduct over a road, the canal is narrowed to half its width. The same amount of water flows downstream of the aqueduct as upstream of it, so at the constriction the water must flow faster. Now, it has been conclusively and complicatedly proved (in Bernoulli's Theorem) that the faster the flow of any fluid, the less pressure is exerted by it on whatever it passes. If that seems illogical, bring an entirely unscientific thought to the problem: imagine the fluid being in such a hurry to go forward that it does not have time to push sideways.

There is another liquid analogy that brings one even closer to the aerofoil situation: if you have no nozzle on your garden hose, what do you do to produce a faster jet of water, without increasing the flow from the tap? You squeeze the end with your thumb, reducing the internal diameter of the pipe at that point. Imagine now that you have squeezed the hose a few inches in from the end. This will produce a rush of water at the constricted point, but by the time it reaches the end, it will be back to normal. If you could isolate that section of the hose that has a depression in the middle, say a foot of it, and if you could then slice that bit of pipe in half horizontally, you would find that the water would still be flowing faster over the bump than anywhere else—despite the fact that nothing is constricting the water from the top. That is exactly what happens over a glider wing.

Consider again that aerofoil section: the upper surface, a curve; the underside, more or less a straight line—and so, of course, a shorter surface than the upper. The same amount of air in front of the wing will very soon be behind it, but the air that passes over the top of the aerofoil has further to go than the air flowing underneath it. The top air has to go faster, it is stretched, and exercises less pressure on the upper surface of the foil than there is pushing on the bottom. Consequently the wing, as long as it moves at an efficient flying speed, is lifted into the area of least pressure.

An efficient flying speed requires an efficient flying angle to the wing. Remember the board in the water? When you twist it up at too great an angle to the direction of travel, you get in trouble—not enough lift, too much drag and a lot of eddies. This angle of inclination to the horizontal (or more accurately, to the direction of the air flow, which is not always the same thing) is known to fliers as the angle of attack. As long as the glider is proceeding efficiently, the air flow both above and below the aerofoil will be smooth and will produce lift. If the angle of attack is increased too much (nose up), the air will pass over the leading edge and become disturbed; instead of a streamlined shape to the air flow, it will be broken into whirls and awkward eddies, just as the water was. Much of the lift is lost, the drag increases and

Executing a turn

the glider begins to stall—that is, it loses so much speed so suddenly that it is no longer an efficient flying machine, but starts to fall out of the sky. The art of design is to see that when this happens the nose drops first and the hang glider begins to gain speed.

The Rogallo type of hang glider (the delta-shaped wing of flexible material) does not suffer from stalling as savagely as does any craft with a more rigid wing. Its flat surface, when inflated by the air pressing underneath it, curves into two gentle, irregular mounds. A section cut through them in flight, at any point, would show conventional aerofoil upper surface. The difference is that if you looked at a number of wing sections parallel to the keel of the Rogallo, you would have a number of aerofoil sections all inclined at different angles to the keel. This makes life rather complicated for the designer of hang gliders. His angle of attack varies from wingtip to wingtip, and so does his dihedral—the angle at which the wings rise above the horizontal across the aircraft; so accepted aircraft design ideas do not apply. The pilot, however, soon discovers these odd shapes do have advantages: the Rogallo, in a stall, behaves with some of the characteristics of a crude parachute. Instead of nose diving or turning over on its back and dropping

In the picture below the ribs show how sections parallel to the keel differ across the wing in flight.

Almost stalling, the pilot now pulls
himself forward to drop the nose.

like a leaf, it is likely that it will drop at an angle that gives the pilot some chance to regain control (by putting the nose down to increase flying speed). And though the drop may be too fast for comfort, it is far less dramatic than it is in other types of hang glider. Given sufficient height at the moment of stall, an experienced Rogallo pilot will usually emerge none the worse for the experience.

At this point observers of the sport will have reached a basic understanding of the potential capabilities of an efficient hang glider in simple conditions. Once in the air, it can attract a sufficient lift force to restrict its drop to a gentle descent as it glides forward. This presumably means that the pilot must launch himself from some sort of a hill, but does it necessarily mean that the only option then open to him is to glide to a landing near the foot of that hill?

Left: a wingtip camera records a group in flight along a hill, but hang gliders can go up hill too, rising on the flowing air, as shown right.

If so, the maximum flight duration is unlikely to be more than a few minutes; but many pilots have stayed aloft more or less all day, and they often land not at the bottom of the hill, but back at the top where they began. So it must be possible for a hang glider to travel upwards, or at least for the pilot to neutralize his descent. To investigate these phenomena is to begin to realize what hang gliding is all about.

A hang glider does travel downwards, but not necessarily in relation to the ground. It moves down in relation to the air flow. What the pilot is constantly seeking is a situation in which the air is moving upwards faster than his rate of sink. Thermals, did you say? That is a term much in use in conventional gliding, when you see the great birds spiralling beautifully upwards on chimneys of warm air. Hang gliders enjoy them too, but find them less often, because of their smaller range of operation. What the hang glider pilot needs is a launching spot at which there is a constant and smooth upward flow of air. He is most likely to find this ideal on a clear hillside, devoid of buildings, rocks or vegetation, and facing either the open sea or an open plain.

Wind moves parallel to the ground. It sweeps unimpeded over the sea or open land and runs up the hills that face it. When it reaches an obstacle (which is unlikely to be streamlined in shape), the wind blows round the sides and over the top and creates turbulence beyond it. When it reaches the top of a hill, it flows, if it can, down the other side. If the hill formation is conducive to it, the wind will form a wave pattern in the air, much as a submerged stone or log in a stream will cause a wave pattern. First comes the wave that marks the position of the obstacle below; and this wave will be repeated several times beyond the stone. If the hill initially hit by the wind is the first of a pair, perhaps of parallel ridges, and if the second ridge occurs just where the repeating air wave is formed, there may be a massive build-up of air waves. For this situation to exist, the air waves must be so spaced that they are flowing upwards when they reach the next hill. If they are not, the waves are destroyed and the air is likely to become extremely turbulent—dangerous conditions for a hang glider.

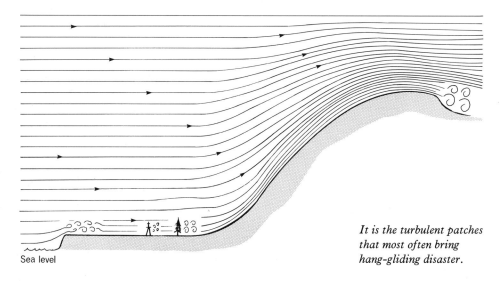

Sea level

It is the turbulent patches that most often bring hang-gliding disaster.

So the pilot is most likely to find success (and safety) by launching into the wind on a smooth slope that faces unbroken land or sea. Even a single hill suitably formed can produce an area of lifting air that extends as much as one-and-a-half times the height of the hill. A cliff is not likely to be suitable, for although there may be an area of strong lift in front of the cliff, its sharp top edge will immediately break the smooth flow and cause eddies into which the glider could be blown back, and from which it is unlikely to escape without being dashed to the ground. Many hang gliding accidents occur in such conditions as these, particularly when the pilot is trying to land on top of a hill over which the air wave pattern is not smooth. A clump of trees will produce

Hilltop landings are hazardous, particularly when unexpected. Windspeed is hard to judge, air waves are often turbulent. The section A-A across the map below is shown left, a nice site for hang gliding, with few problems.

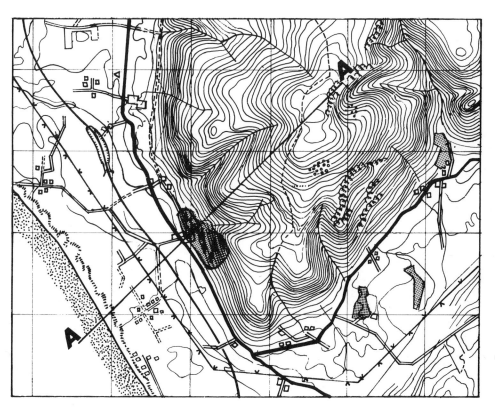

similarly unwelcome problems to the pilot trying to land in its lee; so will a building, where the sharp edges, like those of a cliff, prove particularly irritating to the air flow and can cause conditions in which it is impossible to make a safe landing. Incidentally, it is an oddity worth noting that the ideal hang gliding hill, with a sharpish slope up and a smoothly declining slope on the other side, is almost identical in section to that of a basic aerofoil.

If the direction of the air flow is a hang glider pilot's first concern, its speed comes a close second. As with any other aircraft, each different hang glider is designed for a particular speed range. In the case of an average Rogallo, that will probably be between 15 and 25 mph. Below 15, that hang glider will not fly. If he wants to take off on a windless day, the pilot will have to run at 15 mph in order to leave the ground—an unlikely achievement while you are holding a hang glider over your head. It is more likely that he will wait for a firm and constant breeze of at least 12 mph with the help of which reaching an air speed of 15 is not asking too much. Once airborne, that speed must be maintained, or the craft will stall. Another problem faces the pilot at the top end of his speed range: if his hang glider is not capable of exceeding an air speed of 25 mph and the horizontal component of the air flow into which he is facing is faster than that, then the glider will not be able to fly forward in relation to the ground. The pilot who takes off from the top of a steep hill into a wind of 28 mph will travel upwards all right, but he will also travel backwards, at 3 mph. He is going to be blown back either straight on to the face of the hill, or over the top to an area of turbulence where, even if he avoids a crash, he will find no lift.

So the pilot in search of a flight must carry his glider to a hill of the right shape in the right situation, facing a wind of the right speed. The site itself may not be easy to find, and for the wind all he can do is wait and hope and measure its strength on the instruments that most pilots carry for the purpose, and which you will often see them studying for quite long periods. Air speed when aloft, the rate at which the aircraft and the air flow are passing each other, is something a good hang glider pilot soon learns to sense by the feel of it on his face and by his machine's reaction to it. A Rogallo with a leading edge length of 18 feet may need an air speed of 20 mph or more to develop its best lift.

One other aspect of air flow over the ground is vital to the hang glider pilot, and if we are to understand his problems, it must be mentioned here. You will know that, if you want to enjoy the sun on a breezy day, you will be less troubled by the wind if you lie down than if you sit up; and standing up exposes you to a stronger wind still. This is not just because there may be a useful low windbreak in the vicinity, but because contact with the ground causes friction and actually slows down the speed of the wind. The nearer the ground, the less its force. This phenomenon, known as wind gradient, extends upwards as much as 30 feet, and can have a considerable and sometimes disastrous effect on the landing of a hang glider.

Imagine the pilot just beyond the reach of wind gradient, gliding down at an air speed of 18 mph against a wind of 15 mph. It seems an ideal landing situation, and in a moment or two he will ease the nose up to reduce the speed and induce a controlled stall to drop him gently on the ground. But with every second he is entering more deeply into the arms of wind gradient, and his air speed is dropping much more quickly than he anticipated. At 25 or 30 feet up, the glider stalls—much too soon for a safe landing. The ground hits him uncompromisingly hard. Because of wind gradient, the hang glider pilot must be sure that he increases his speed relative to the ground as he comes in to land.

At the last moment of his descent, the pilot meets another strange air condition. Air becomes trapped between the wing and the ground, giving him the feeling that he is landing on a cushion of air. This is known as 'ground effect', and helps to slow the rate of fall in the final few feet. Experienced pilots use the same condition to their advantage when they are trying to achieve the longest possible glide. They fly as close to the ground as they dare

at quite a high speed, trusting in that unseen cushion (and their own fine handling of the hang glider) to keep them from actually touching the ground. Think of a hovercraft: that is the ultimate use of ground effect—helped, of course, by the man-made downward thrust from the engines.

We have not said much so far about the way a pilot controls his machine. It could hardly be simpler: all changes of direction in a hang glider—up, down

Daring use of 'ground effect', a cushion of air.

Steering? All done by weight change. Shift the body, alter the centre of gravity, and the glider rolls with you.

or sideways—are brought about by the pilot changing the position of his own body in the craft, and thus changing its centre of gravity. In the early hang gliders, the pilot was not secured by a harness. He did not even have a seat. All he could do to hang on to the flying wing was to hook his arms over a pair of parallel bars that ran fore and aft under the keel. With those nestling hard in his armpits, he was up and away. Control? That was achieved by swinging his feet, forwards or backwards, this side or that.

The same principle applies today, but it is rather safer and a lot more comfortable. Secure in his harness, or sitting in his swinging seat, the pilot's hands rest on the control bar, the bottom member of what used to be called the 'A' frame. In the most stable and well-balanced gliders, no pressure on the bar should be needed for normal flight (if it is, on a long flight the strength the pilot needs for manoeuvring will be sapped). To change direction, the pilot moves the control bar one way or another, which has the same effect as his shifting the weight of his body on those parallel bars: it changes the centre of gravity of the craft, since the weight force always acts on that point. (The lift force acts on the centre of pressure, which is not quite the same thing, but a point determined by the original design and the angle of attack of the moment; the drag force, operating against the direction of travel, may not act constantly over the whole craft—a flag flown from the king post, for example, will increase drag at the top but not at the bottom, changing the flying characteristics of that machine.)

A moment of tension: as one pilot pulls out of a sharp, diving turn, the other moves to the left.

Changing the point of action of any of these forces will alter the attitude of the glider, but in practice most gliders are controlled just by changing the centre of gravity. When the pilot pushes the control bar to the left, his weight moves the centre of gravity to the right; the hang glider begins to roll to the right, and then to turn to the right. (Technically this is known as a roll-induced yaw.) For aerodynamic reasons, to explain which is beyond the intended scope of this book, the pilot pushes the bar away from him during the turn if he wants to increase the rate at which he is turning, and pulls it towards him to decrease the rate. If he did not have sufficient speed when he entered the turn, he would be likely to suffer a considerable drop in height during the manoeuvre.

A further complication that can arise is that the inside wing of the turn travels more slowly than the outside one; so if the pilot is not going into the turn with sufficient speed, a stall on that side is more than likely. On the other hand, as he comes out of the turn, the pilot must push the bar away from him, to decrease speed and level the flight out again. A diving turn might result if he did not, at a speed that would be dangerous at low altitude. As you can see, turning should be altogether a very precisely co-ordinated business: the right entry speed, the roll and increase of speed, the easing up of the nose to restore stable flight.

One last thought while you are watching this manoeuvre: the sharper the turn, the more likely a stall; and the sharper the turn, the more acute the pressure of the centrifugal force, which during the turn causes the pilot's weight to swing out sideways against it. At a banking angle of 60 degrees, the load on the airframe doubles. If the pilot has to bank as sharply as 84 degrees, the load increases to ten times the normal. If structural failure is ever going to come, that is likely to be the moment.

We have tried in this chapter to explain why and how a hang glider flies. Please do not interpret anything we have said as if it were an instruction manual. There is only one way to learn to fly safely, and that is with an instructor. Some of the saddest and most frequent accidents in this sport occur to people who believe they can manage with, so to speak, a book in one hand and the control frame in the other. In hang gliding there must be no such thing as do-it-yourself—as the following pages painfully demonstrate.

Forced into making a turn too close to the hillside, this pilot is about to learn his lesson the hard way. His flying speed is lost, the ground will win.

A man looking for agony :
Henri Bayard looping in Switzerland.

5 Coming Down

Too many people have been killed hang gliding. Two would be too many, and between 1971 and 1976 there were more than 100—with the global spread of the sport, finding accurate figures is almost impossible. Does that make it a dangerous sport? The public, and certainly the Press, would not hesitate to answer 'Yes'. We prefer to suggest that the sport is loaded with potential hazards, very few of which are likely to cause serious harm provided they are approached sensibly and handled carefully: it is carelessness that kills, not hang gliders.

Look at that power point in the corner of your room: a death-dealing instrument. It will kill a baby who stuffs wet little fingers into the holes, but it will never kill you. Being aware of its harmful potential, you respect it. Nor will a train kill you, unless you are foolish enough to try and get across the line in front of it.

An analysis of hang gliding accidents reported in Britain in 1975 (of which three were fatal) shows that 48 per cent occurred to pilots who had made thirteen or fewer flights; 23 per cent happened on the first or second flight. The statistics for 1974 are even more revealing: while 54 per cent of reported accidents were suffered by pilots with fewer than ten flights to their credit, 80 per cent occurred to pilots who had never made a flight that lasted as long as ten minutes. After striking the novice so forcibly, the accident rate declines as experience is gained, until there comes a remarkable leap in the graph after thirty flights. Strongly allied to that statistic arises another: 28 per cent of all accidents in 1975 happened to pilots making their first flight from that particular site.

Translating the facts into human terms, you can presume that the most dangerous hang-glider pilot is the uninformed and over-confident beginner who, in the words of one expert, 'steps off a cliff without realising he is in a flying machine'. Coming along fast as a hazard is the pilot of some experience who reckons he is now smart enough to beat the train across the tracks, but is in fact not sensible enough to discover, before he makes his run, that there is a tripwire in the middle. There are old pilots and there are bold pilots, but there are no pilots both old and bold.

In the United States of America, the fatal accident figures are terrifying; but remember this is a nation of two hundred million people, of whom perhaps 25,000 are hang-glider pilots. Statistics for road accidents read like a world war casualty list, and even the number of accidents with lawn mowers seems incredible to the rest of the world. In 1974, the worst year to date, forty-two pilots were killed. What was particularly appalling was that of the sixty-one who took part in the National Hang Gliding Championships in October, 1973, five were dead within thirteen months. They had perhaps, as someone suggested, become so good they were bored by 'safe' flying.

Examining in detail some of the 1975 American fatalities, one finds facts to support that hypothesis. We picked a block of twelve at random from the list: three were caused by complex manoeuvres beyond the capability of the pilot, and/or the glider. Five others were attributed to machine failure, three being in gliders unfit to fly; one pilot was electrocuted on power lines to which he had drifted while taking photographs; one was flying in impossibly bad conditions; one was wearing a faulty harness; and one, apparently wearing no harness at all, simply fell out of his seat. It seems that ten of those twelve deaths could have been avoided if the pilots had been more responsible and more careful—and one of them, we noted with horror, was only twelve years old.

Freak fatal accidents do occasionally happen. A Swiss pilot, forced by lack of head wind to run too fast and too far to take off, stumbled in a ditch and broke his neck. An experienced Briton put his machine into a fatal dive when a hook on his boot became entangled with the rigging wire. An American, knocked out when he crashed in a tree, was choked to death by the blood that ran out of a head wound. And the sport will not forget the awful lesson of the pilot whose well-meaning friends, when he broke his thigh, took him sixty miles in the back of a van so that he would be treated at a hospital near his home. He died.

Whatever its nature, every serious accident in a hang glider provides a story for the Press and ammunition for the critics. The sport in Britain experienced its very worst eight days in July, 1976: a very experienced male pilot and an inexperienced female both died, the latter some days after receiving terrible injuries; three other fliers, one of them a girl pupil under instruction, broke bones; and one man had a spectacular crash into a car park, injuring a spectator and damaging two cars. Two Members of Parliament promptly called for a public enquiry into the sport, and a ban on it meanwhile. The Royal Society for the Prevention of Accidents, pointing out that there were forty or fifty hang-gliding accidents a year in Britain (an under-estimate), asked for legislation to control it.

Reporters called at a Sussex hospital near the hang-gliding action, where the consultant added fuel to the raging fire: 'This is a very dangerous sport. We have treated thirty hang-gliding injuries in the past six months—more than all other sporting injuries put together.' The injuries had included a broken spine producing paralysis, and many broken arms, which he thought indicated a fault in hang-gliding design. What it does in fact indicate is man's natural tendency to thrust out his arms to break his fall. We have analysed all the accidents reported to the British Hang Gliding Association over a period of eighteen months (and the Association constantly urges its members to make such reports). There were 130, of which thirty-five resulted in no injury at all, and thirty in minor injuries—cuts, grazes, sprains, bruises. Five were fatal, and the remaining sixty pilots all suffered broken bones. Fractured wrists were the most common (14), and there were more legs (12) than arms (10) or ankles (7). There were two fractures of the pelvis and five of the spine.

Assuming that only members of the BHGA report their accidents to the Association, and that all members make an equal number of flights, then in one year (and in round figures), one member in thirty is likely to have an accident, one in forty-five will be injured, and one in seventy will break a bone. Nobody should pretend that such figures are insignificant, but they do not look particularly savage compared with the toll taken, for instance, by American football. Fifteen dead in 1975, and that is in hand-to-hand combat; anybody who plays the game throughout his high school and college life has a 95 per cent chance, it is said, of serious injury. And in sleepy old Britain, six people were killed playing cricket in 1975.

That Sussex doctor's cry was balanced a few weeks later by one from a medical officer in the south-western county of Devonshire, who at the time when hang gliding was under fire wrote to his local authority to point out that in his hospital they treat more accidents caused by horse riding (most of them broken bones or head injuries) than by all other activities put together—including motoring, motor cycling, swimming, boating, hang gliding, walking, cricket and football. 'My own partner broke his back not long ago in a fall from a horse. If it had been a hang glider, without doubt it would have been reported in the national Press. But that does not mean I would like to ban horse riding, and I hope no one else would want to. The point I am making is that just because a recreation is unquestionably dangerous, as riding and hang gliding are, is not sufficient reason to oppose it. Hang-glider pilots are not irresponsible or thoughtless (unlike many motorists) and the element of risk is a part of their enjoyment, just as it is in rock climbing or mountaineering.'

The secretary of the BHGA, under pressure, went so far as to say that anything that was worth doing was dangerous—a remark open to challenge.

The picture above shows the nose of a kite being held steady just before take-off.

About one accident in four happens to a pilot on his first or second flight, usually when panic needlessly sets in. The earliest steps can be taken in a tethered glider, with the instructor keeping the kite within a few feet of the ground. If the pupil loses control, he (or she) is pulled down to earth— maybe with a bruise, but not with a fracture.

He went on: 'If people are free to go up Everest and fall off, why go on at us?' No doubt the answer to that lies in man's basic conviction that whatever madness we perpetrate on the ground is natural, whatever gentle sanity we exercise in the air is something that God did not mean us to do. Thus the man who falls under a train—and many do—rates a paragraph at the bottom of the page, while the sporting parachutist who meets a tragic end is awarded bold treatment. The motor racing driver who dies in flames is a hero, the hang glider pilot is a fool.

In actuarial terms, the insurance industry rates a hang-glider pilot a better risk than a ski-er and several times better than a skin diver. In reaching this conclusion, they will no doubt have investigated these three prime sources of danger in the sport: the man, his machine and the air in which they fly. The hang glider itself may be of basically unsound design, leading to structural failure or dangerous handling characteristics; in Britain, as in several other countries, the national association tries to prevent this by an inspection system agreed with the manufacturers. It may have been made from material of poor quality, a hazard over which the manufacturer has little control, since he can neither produce all the parts himself nor test all those he buys.

The hang glider may have deteriorated with age, or harsh wear, or poor handling—and it deteriorates more quickly on the roof rack of a car than anywhere else. Unless the rack is extended as far as possible fore and aft, the

Never try to do it yourself—the only safe way to learn is with an instructor. This one gently talks sense into the one-way radio. His pupil (far left) gets the message loud and clear in his helmet.

unsupported two-thirds of the eighteen feet of aluminium tubing flexes wildly as the car moves. And lastly, it may be poorly maintained, or inadequately checked, by the pilot. For instance, some pilots fail to keep caps over the open ends of the tubing that forms the machine's skeleton. One such allowed more and more earth to become wedged up the rear of his keel tube, where it hit the ground on landing, and the weight of it caused the machine to fly more nose-up than it used to. Unaware of what was causing that, the pilot adjusted the trim of the craft accordingly. One day, discovering the mud but still not associating it with flight characteristics, he dug it all out with a screwdriver, took off and promptly nose-dived to the ground.

It should be as unnecessary to remind a pilot of the hazards of the fluid medium he is flying in as to point out to a car driver that there is ice on the road, or oil, or broken glass; but many untutored novices ignore the perils of airflow, and some experienced fliers regard such perils as a challenge to their skill. It is almost impossible to fly safely in turbulent conditions, whether they are created by the permanent physical characteristics of the site, or by the changing weather conditions of the day. While experience soon teaches one to recognize the former, the latter is still an area to which many pilots pay insufficient attention. Education in basic meteorology is as essential for the hang glider pilot as it is for the mountaineer, and a lot easier; it may be difficult to predict the weather six hours from now, but what is coming to you in twenty minutes should be no secret.

As to the pilot himself as a potential hazard, it is clear that his stupidity, ignorance and lack of care can contribute greatly to the hazards put in his way by both machine and nature; but the man as a pilot is largely at the mercy of his own conceit. He puts himself at risk by failing to recognize his own limitations—and sometimes, like many a car driver, by failing to consider that the guy coming from the other direction may be even less competent. There are times when he will be unexpectedly faced with unfair hazards, but the unexpected is what all pilots must expect. There may be power lines that he could not see when he took off, or barbed wire fences that only appear when he is about to land on them. Small children and large dogs he needs to avoid at both ends of the flight, and model aircraft in the middle of it. The turbulence caused by a helicopter passing overhead is immense, and that from a jet aircraft spreads, and can take twenty minutes to disperse.

When all is said and accounted for, thoughtlessness and over-confidence are the killers. You can make a mistake when you are sailing and get away with it. You can be a mad motorist and remain protected by your steel armour. But if you get it wrong in a hang glider, retribution is swift and spectacular. Aviation in itself is not dangerous, somebody wrote long ago. But to an even greater degree than the sea, it is terribly unforgiving of any carelessness, incapacity or neglect.

Rogallos are also built with dual control—two harnesses and a wider control frame—which has all the advantages of the similar arrangement on the roads. The apprehensive pupil can experience flight without having to take responsibility for it and can gradually ease into the sensations of control with the secure comfort beside her that will banish panic.

Dan Poynter

6 The American Experience

Modern hang gliding starts with Rogallo, the man whose name is almost daily on the lips of every hang glider pilot in the world. Even now, thirty years after he created the portable, folding, flexible wing that was half kite and half parachute—and was nearly used to retrieve space capsules from orbit—he remains more celebrated in the sport than any later designer, than the greatest pilots. He did not build the first hang glider, nor fly the first, but like Henry Ford, he produced the machine that lit a flame around the globe. Hang gliding now takes place in at least fifty countries, and in such as Australia, France and the United Kingdom has expanded at an astonishing speed. But the United States of America remains its home, with by far the greatest number of exponents of the sport. From here, Dan Poynter contributes this expert and detailed history of its development.

Francis Melvin Rogallo has carved a niche in the annals of hang gliding not as a pilot or builder, but because his kite has been adapted and is the most popular form of hang glider seen in the air today. Rogallo was born in 1912 in Sanger, in the middle of California, and as a child often flew kites. Recalling his youth, he said: 'When I was seven years old, an airplane flew over our town and I decided to make aeronautics my career. When I was 13, I saved enough money to buy a ride in a dilapidated Curtiss Jenny over Fresno, without first discussing the possibility with my parents. Today, I probably wouldn't fly in the same airplane if it were free.' Rogallo went on to graduate from Stanford University in 1935 with a degree in mechanical-aero engineering and worked briefly for Shell Chemical and Douglas Aircraft. Then he moved on to Hampton, Virginia, and the Langley Laboratory, later the Research Center of the National Advisory Committee for Aeronautics, where he was in charge of the Full-scale Research Division of the Low Speed Vehicle Branch. In 1939 he married Gertrude Sugden, who later shared in his work. (The patent for the Rogallo wing was taken out in the names of them both.)

The point of no return : Marvin Drewry about to step off Stoney Man into the Shenandoah Valley, Virginia. This is the moment when faint hearts yearn for a nice game of chess at home, rye on the rocks, and hamburgers to follow. What a fine mess you got me into, pal!

Dan Poynter

Rogallo recalled: 'At the close of the Second World War, we thought the NACA should initiate research that would give the average citizen a better opportunity to fly by developing a more practical and less expensive airplane. The NACA decided not to undertake such a project, so Gertrude and I decided to work on it at home in our own time. One of our goals was to develop an inexpensive rugged wing that could be folded easily when the aircraft was on the ground—like a bird or bat folds his wings.'

Their experimental work resulted in the patent application in 1948 (granted in 1951) for their 'flexible kite'. The preamble to the specification on the patent reads as follows:

> This invention relates to kites and more particularly to a kite having completely flexible surfaces.
>
> It is an object of our invention to provide a kite of simple and economic construction and wherein the use of reinforcing members may be ordinarily eliminated.
>
> It is another object of our invention to provide a kite which will be simple to fly and graceful in flight.
>
> It is a further object of our invention to provide a structure for a kite having improved aerodynamic characteristics.
>
> In general we achieve the above object by constructing a kite of a substantially quadrilateral piece of fabric, paper or other light and flexible material, having bridle strings attached at various points, and a tail secured to the kite when necessary, so that the stress in the strings exerted at strategic points of the kite's surface maintains the kite in

Nobody does it this way for too long, unless he has the grip of a gorilla and plastic armpits. In Australia and the United States, a lot of guys with flat kites were towed on water-skies behind motor boats, giving them lift-off without the sweat of climbing a hill.

proper shape and configuration to be effectively supported even in a light breeze. Owing to the fact that our kite does not require the use of stiffening members, it is considerably lighter than other kites of the same area and hence more easily flown in a light breeze.

Though all of that relates only to a kite flown on an anchor line, the last page of the Rogallo patent application contains this interesting extract:

Further, we believe the principle described herein may be applied to man-carrying devices, such as airplanes, parachutes and gliders, and in such event stabilizing and control surfaces could be added.

Long before this, some special circumstances arose that awoke the dormant sport of hang gliding in the United States. Early in the war, in 1941, the Government banned all flying within 150 miles of the California coast. A frustrated enthusiast, Volmer Jensen, built a nice, quiet hang glider that had three axis controls and actually flew. During the next thirty-plus years he built more than a score of gliders, powered planes and amphibians. His modern hang gliders are some of the best-designed and most professionally produced.

In 1951, the then 30 year-old-sport of water ski-ing was enlivened with the addition of the flat kite. In 1957, Rollie Bonneau learned of the flat kite in France and took it home to Ontario. That same year, an Australian, Doug Leivshaw, introduced it to the famed water ski show park in Florida, Cypress Gardens. The kites were flat in design, similar to a toy paper kite. The flyer would hang on to the cross bar as if he were 'chinning' himself. The length of time he remained in the air depended on just how long he had the strength to hang on. The first kites were not aerodynamically designed, so the altitude of their flight was mostly determined by how much the flyer pushed off as he skied over the water ski jump. They soon became more sophisticated and a wild Floridian named Ken Tibado directed his talents towards building and flying them, winning the first World Kite Championships at Cypress Gardens in 1957. With the addition of a swing harness, the flying became less strenuous, certain trick manoeuvres became possible, and the pendulum action of the new suspension made the system more stable.

Later refinements allowed 'hands-off' flying and control of the kite's lateral movement by moving a bar. A boat-end release allowed the observer in the boat to jettison the flyer if he got into trouble; the kite would react as an air brake and settle into the water. Flat kite flying became easy and reasonably safe, and before the end of 1957, Alphonso Woodall of Cleveland was towed all the way across Lake Erie to Canada, demonstrating that kiting was not a momentary feat.

The water skiers soon adapted the flat kite to their slalom course; they would swing the bar to tilt the kite and fly around the buoys on each side of the course. Then certain gymnastic routines performed on the bar developed into another event called 'tricks' and competition began. The American Water Ski Association began sanctioning kiting tournaments.

In 1958, Sputnik was launched and the United States suddenly found itself in the space race. Interest renewed in the Rogallo kite principle; they were air dropped, towed and motorized. Millions of dollars were spent by NASA (National Aeronautics and Space Administration) and the armed services on trying to develop them into useful vehicles. A great deal of basic research and testing was done, and reams of reports were printed. NASA built and flew the Paresev test vehicle, while the US Army and Ryan Aircraft Co. developed and flight-tested a variety of towed gliders for aerial delivery of cargo and equipment. Some were so stable that no guiding was necessary from lift off to touch down. Some were released at altitude and radio-controlled to a predetermined landing point. With the simple attachment of a flexible wing, several ground vehicles, including a jeep, were towed aloft.

All this activity and the resulting publicity stimulated the thought of people all over the world. One was Barry Hill Palmer, who writes of his work in 1961: 'I had been working on man-powered aircraft and other aero absurdities when two people where I worked at Aerojet General, in Nimbus, California, came to see me independently and showed me a magazine photograph of Ryan's first powered flex wing. I don't know whose light went on or whose buzzer went off, but the conclusion was that a hang glider could be built. I sized up the wing and studied its performance, using a digital computer, in late 1961. But as you know, ideas are cheap and it's the doing

There were many attempts to make more practical use of flexible delta wing principles. Below: a Rogallo-type parachute and, right, the intriguing powered Ryan Flex Wing: 'the craziest kite in the sky', 1962.

that counts. The first wing I built was a 22 footer. Analytical studies indicated that the 80 degree apex angle then used on Rogallo wings was too narrow, so it was opened up to a conservative 90 degrees. I was concerned about the very problems in pitch that are now doing-in some of the fliers. My first wing, in its final development, was the wing that re-started hang gliding. It performed quite well, after a learning period required to fly an aircraft that was not guaranteed to fly. By 1962, three of us, John Spealman, Kenneth Clarke and myself were flying the wing and then John went on to build the black wing using first class construction and a $130 cost to match. Mine cost little over $10.

Typical flights were started with sort of a hop, landing, a skip and the flight. Why I would make the preliminary jump, I don't know, but everyone else did the identical thing. The flight would usually run some 120 yards.

Today, this sort of operation is reckoned as part of water-skiing and not of hang gliding.

The longest, which resulted in some very sore and tired underarms, was over 200 yards. The aircraft flew at around 10 to 15 feet altitude but gusts would lift it much higher, to a maximum of 80 feet. Later on I developed a fully-flared landing into the wind with essentially zero forward speed. Things became more interesting when we discovered that we could land the wing at zero forward speed in zero headwind, quite a feat for a fixed wing aircraft.' So Barry Palmer was the first to foot-launch a Rogallo wing, an historic moment in the development of hang gliding.

The first swing seat came around 1963. Rather than borrow the swing that the water skiers were using with their kites, Palmer fashioned a ski-lift type of seat and mounted it to the wing with a home-made universal joint. A single stick projected down from the wing and carried the wing structural support. He later went on to build and fly some very successful powered versions.

In North Carolina in 1961 Tom Purcell, Jr, towed aloft a Rogallo wing, to which he added floats and flew behind a boat. In 1963, John Dickenson, an Australian engineer known as the 'Father of Kiting', was the first water skier to put down his flat kite and try a Rogallo. He found that the delta-shaped kite's altitude could be varied by changing the angle at which it flew. It was Dickenson who introduced the Rogallo to fellow-Australian water-ski kitemen Bill Bennett and Bill Moyes, who continued to fly the product he designed and built. At first the flat-kite advocates ostracized the delta, and then tried to force it into the mould of the flat kite competition. But soon the Rogallo was found to be more versatile; it could be released at altitude to glide back down to a landing. It was a whole new concept. The new Rogallo flyers preferred free flight to the captive tow line and many lost interest in competing with flat kites.

One of the most famous creations in the history of the sport:
Richard Miller's original Bamboo Butterfly, right; and a
later model, below.

Richard Miller

At about this time, another of the memorable names of hang gliding emerged: Richard Miller, who was to build and fly the 'Bamboo Butterfly'. In an early edition of the American magazine *Low, Slow and Out of Control* he wrote: 'It was during an idyllic six weeks on Cape Cod in the autumn of 1962, much of it spent climbing on the great dunes that face the Atlantic, that the urge to build a hang glider once again rose to the surface.' That winter he learned the basic details of a Rogallo wing, and the following summer built a design study of one.

I was running a parachute loft at the Oakland Airport when in walked Miller in early 1964 searching for materials for his 'Bamboo Butterfly'. This particularly literate sky dreamer knew where he was going, but I am not sure he knew how he was going to get there. He was intensely interesting and we talked of numerous forms of aviation. He returned again about three weeks later all battered and bruised and announced: 'I'm learning how to fly!' His craft was mostly bamboo reinforced with fibreglass, and a six-millimetre polyethylene sail, twelve feet square with grommets along the side for attachment. The crossbar was a warren-truss affair. Later Miller went on to become editor of *Soaring* magazine, to do a great deal of writing and to inspire many others to dream and fly.

Others were equally impressed with the Rogallo concept, among them the US Government, who in July 1963 presented the inventors with the largest cash award ever made by NASA for a scientific contribution. (Rogallo recalls: 'This award was contested by the Internal Revenue Service, however, and after final settlement ten years later, the Federal and State income taxes and interest and legal expenses just about equalled the amount of the award.') During the space race in 1966, NASA was working on three deployable gliders for manned spacecraft recovery: The Rogallo Para Wing, the Jalbert Para Foil and the Barish Sail Wing. They were in a hurry and they poured in the money. (There is a story that compares NASA's approach to development with making nine women pregnant—in order to produce a baby in one month.) Dave Barish foot-launched his sail wing as a testing method. I worked for Barish at the time, tried the wing, liked it and wrote about it. The army looked into a personnel version of the delta wing and several were quickly produced by Pioneer Parachute Co. and Irvin Industries for tests. Irvin went on to manufacture them and they were marketed to the sport through Steve Snyder Enterprises as the 'Delta II Para Wing' in 1969.

Another to have read some NASA reports, and to have heard of Barry Palmer's work, was Jim Natland, but he was not aware of any other Rogallo activity. He is credited with building and flying the first Rogallo hang glider made of aircraft-type materials, which he did in Rolling Hills, southern California. The glider is now on display at the Aerospace Museum, Balboa Park, San Diego. In 1966–7, he moved his activities to the tenth green of the Huntsville Golf Course in Alabama. He says of his flying: 'I worked alone on it for about two years and was pretty much ridiculed by spectators and became kind of a local nut because of it.' Natland made many long ground skimming flights; often 150 feet long and between three and seven feet high.

In 1967, Bill Moyes launched on snow skis from Australia's Mount Crackenback and glided more than five miles, for another of the sport's 'firsts'. Then he released from 1,000 feet after a tow lift. Bill Bennett, who worked with Moyes, brought the first water ski Rogallo kite to the US in April, 1969, while Moyes took his kite and toured Europe. Dave Kilbourne, a water skier/kiter, met Bennett at Marine World and provided the boat for several demonstration flights in San Francisco Bay. Bennett went on to tour the US and then decided to settle and start a kite manufacturing business in the Los Angeles area. Bennett's kite was smaller and it supported the flyer in a seat, while most of the foot-launched people were hanging by their arms from parallel bars and shifting their weight to guide their craft. It never occurred to them to control the kite any other way. Dave Kilbourne, recognizing the superiority of the Australian water ski kite control system, took the glider out and foot-launched it. He became the first to foot-launch a Rogallo with the triangular control frame and swing seat system.

Two of the great pioneers, both Australian water-tow enthusiasts who came to the States: Bill Bennett and Bill Moyes. Both kites use floats; Moyes, above, has extra buoyancy on the keel tip.

Later in 1969, Moyes became the first to soar. He foot-launched near Sydney and stayed aloft some 32 minutes, flying back and forth on the uprising air. Also that same year, he towed to 2,870 feet over Lake Ellesmere in New Zealand on 12,000 feet of cable payed out from a winch. After Bennett's early 1970 visit to Cypress Gardens, the Rogallo glider displaced the flat kite in the four-times-daily ski show. Bennett demonstrated the flying ability of the new kite by climbing up behind the ski boat to release and go into free flight. After several fantastic manoeuvres, he made a perfect landing on the beach, to everyone's amazement.

All this time, Terry Sweeney was building and gliding biplanes in the mountains of New Hampshire; more than a dozen of them. He had no knowledge of the flying being done in the 'outside world'. He thought he was the only one. It was Tom Peghiny who 'rescued' him and turned him on to Rogallos. Tom and Terry continued to work together designing better gliders. It was 6 September, 1971, when Dave Kilbourne foot-launched

The most technically advanced hang gliders use wings that are more rigid than flexible, making folding and transport difficult. These are all models of the Icarus developed by Taras Kiceniuk, shown left in the harness of an Icarus V.

from Mission Peak, near San Francisco, to soar for 1 hour 4 minutes. Taras Kiceniuk quickly followed in his Icarus I biplane. Jack Lambie sponsored a hang-gliding meeting on 23 October, 1971, to honour the birthday of Otto Lilienthal. It brought numerous enthusiasts and some incredible machines together; the movement gathered momentum. Volmer Jensen watched the take-offs (and crashes) and returned for consultations with Irv Culver. The VJ-23, a cantilevered monoplane with three-axis control, was the result.

Below and at the top of the picture, right, another high-performance glider, Volmer Jensen's VJ-23 in a 90 minute flight over Torrano Beach, California, the 62 year old designer at the controls.

Mont Blanc is 15,766 feet high. About the same altitude is Rudy Kishazy in 1973, with skis and ski sticks in case of need.

In the early 70's the race was on to see who could go the highest or furthest. In 1970, Bob Kennedy launched from a balloon over Lake Elsinore, California. The next year, Bennett towed to 2,960 feet on a 7,000 feet polyethylene boat-winched line over Lake Havasu in Arizona, in conjunction with the reopening of the transplanted London Bridge. Then Moyes airplane-towed to 8,610 feet over Amery, Wisconsin. Next, Kilbourne balloon-launched from 9,200 feet. In 1972, Moyes towed to 4,750 feet over Lake Ellesmere behind a 70 mph jet boat. Later, Bennett and Kennedy made the first two-man flight on the 'Duo-Delta' for a half mile in Mission Bay, San Diego.

The United States Hang Gliding Association began as the 25 member Peninsula Hang Gliding Club in December, 1971, under the leadership of Dick Eipper. It soon attracted membership from neighbouring areas and early in 1972 became the Southern California Hang Gliding Association. A monthly publication, *Ground Skimmer*, started in May of that year. Begun as a news vehicle for the membership, it soon grew to be a comprehensive recording of movement history, technical articles and so on. Though it was probably the first club publication, *Ground Skimmer* was not the first magazine for the hang glider pilot. *Low, Slow and Out of Control* was the first published in March, 1967, but it only survived for six issues. In March, 1971, Joe Faust began publishing a monthly, *Low and Slow*. Subsequent national publicity resulted in an explosion of memberships. By the end of 1973, more

Once in a lifetime? The world's biggest hot-air balloon (310 feet tall) lifts eight Eipper Performance Cumulus VBs, designed by 1975 world champion David Cronk, for a mass drop over California. Cronk is the pilot bottom centre of the picture.

than 5,000 were on the rolls and the organization had become truly national in scope. The name was changed to the United States Hang Gliding Association and membership passed 10,000. (There are at the time of writing at least 25,000 hang glider pilots in the States.)

Modern hang gliding began to be publicly noticed when a regular 20-foot sand flying site was established in 1972 at Playa del Rey, on the edge of Los Angeles. To quote Bill Allen: 'It was like any other day, except that if you were at Playa del Rey that weekend in May 1972, you would have seen an unusual assortment of strange flying craft. It was a slice out of the 'old days' of hang gliding, but it also came as growing popularity was changing the sport. Soon it would be no longer just for tinkerers and people simply interested in the joy of creativity and flight. Instead, popularity would bring the availability of plans, kits and even complete, ready-to-fly gliders. And with these would come commercialism, with both its benefits and vexations. But on this sunny day, nobody looked at your tee shirt to see what company you were associated with. Nobody criticized your surplus tubing, bamboo, plastic or baling wire. And there was only shared laughter when the aeronauts went home with more pieces than they brought. It was assumed they would be back in a few days with repaired or new gliders—ones which probably would fly better anyway.'

One day that year, the media happened on these happy weekend flyers and suddenly the local Los Angeles pastime excited the nation. George Uveges and Bill Allen supplied the photographs. Between Joe Faust and the SCHGA, people had places to write for more information. Thousands of letters poured in. Information went out and the sport exploded! As more and more people became excited about hang gliding and jumped in (off?) to pioneer the new sport, accidents began to happen at an alarming rate. People were towing kites with automobiles, snowmobiles, dune buggies, motorcycles or often just an eager bunch of helpers at the other end of the rope. Often they didn't know how to water ski, drive a boat, fly a glider and many did not even make initial towing trials over water. Tow lines were breaking, kites were diving into the ground, and there were structural failures. Footlaunched hang gliding was no safer; it too was expanding faster than the instruction. Anyone could buy a mail order kite—and they did. Anyone could build them—and they did. Anyone could open a school—and they did! The foot-launched kites were not designed for the stresses of towing and their manufacturers justifiably warned against it. The accidents continued and the American Water Ski Association withdrew its support and sanction of any kind, asking the flyers to form their own organization. The SCHGA stood by its Bye-laws and recommended foot-launch only. In some countries, hang gliding is still part of the water ski group.

It was not until mid-1975 that knowledge caught up with enthusiasm and

*Is there no end to it? Bill Bennett (still clad
ready for water) takes a trip attached to a car.*

Aussie Steve Moyes (son of Bill) about to release his Dragonfly from a tow over Cypress Gardens, Florida, home of much hang gliding competition.

the fatality rate began a welcome decline. Significantly, this coincided with a shake-out in the industry. Purchasers would not settle for just anything that flew. It had to be safe and fly well; they knew the difference. Many manufacturers, schools and dealers closed their doors.

Harry Robb, a retired Air Force colonel, is credited with reunifying foot-launch and tow-launch hang gliding in the US. A well-known water ski judge, Robb directed the Rogallo tow-kite championships at Cypress Gardens. He drafted the competition regulations and set an example for foot-launch. He invited me to judge the 1974 meet. They were so exciting I wrote a book on the sport entitled *Manned Kiting*. Robb wrote articles, educated the USHGA Board of Directors and was eventually successful in having the Bye-law towing exclusion removed. During this time, he was elected to the USHGA Board, was appointed alternate delegate to the Commission Internationale de Vol Libre (Hang Gliding) of the Fédération Aéronautique Internationale, and was then elected Secretary to that body.

In the design field, all were startled by Roy Haggard's truncated-tip Dragonfly glider at the January 1975 Nationals at Escape Country. He and his design went to work for Ultralite Products and he demonstrated the new craft to the world at the Alpine Championships in Kossen, Austria, in March. Everyone returned to their drawing boards. Many still thought that tow-kites had to be smaller and that battens were only used to keep poorly-tailored sails quiet. There was a design revolution going on. Early in 1976, gliders with battened radial wing tips made their debut. They were so much more stable in pitch that all previous gliders without the special tips were pronounced dangerous. Through the early seventies, many rigid wings were developed but none sold terribly well. The basic Rogallo shape could always be redesigned to improve the performance far more easily than a rigid could be designed for portability. And Francis Rogallo, retired in Kitty Hawk, North Carolina, smiles and makes another flight.

7 Echoes around the World

Hang gliding grows so fast it is difficult to keep track of the number of its followers even in your own country. A survey in 1975 suggested there were 40,000 hang gliders in the world, of which 25,000 were in the USA. France and the United Kingdom jostled for second place, sharing 6,000, but subsequently Australia claims to have overtaken them both. The speed with which the sport has grown is dramatically illustrated by the situation in Britain, where the first issue of *The Illustrated Monthly Fly Paper* in November, 1973, supposed there were fewer than a hundred fliers in the whole country.

A month later, the National Hang Gliding Association (of which *Fly Paper* was the organ) reported 585 members. In January there were 872, in February 1,130. By May the figure was 1,600 and in November nearly 3,000—an increase, if they were right in the first estimate, of a staggering 2,000 per cent in a year; and an accurate one of 500 per cent in Association members in eleven months.

A second national organization, the British Kite Soaring Association, was formed at the end of 1973, and the NHGA almost immediately began to woo them into amalgamation. They proved to be somewhat reluctant brides. At this time, the NHGA was run virtually single-handed by one enthusiast, John James, and it was not until December, 1974, that a new and more democratic association, the British Hang Gliding Association, was formed from the membership of the two existing bodies. (By that time the Scottish Sailwing Association had come into being, but it chose to remain independent until the beginning of 1977, when it joined the BHGA.)

The executive of the new association settled swiftly to serious work, and the monthly magazine changed its name to *Wings* and took a more responsible attitude to its members and the sport. Hitherto the prevailing atmosphere had been understandably light-hearted, if not positively Monty Pythonesque. By the end of the year the Association had drawn up codes of

Hang gliding around the world: Above: S. Wales.

Top right : Japan,   lower right : New Zealand.

conduct for flying and for behaviour on sites; had negotiated with land-owners for the use of sites; devised an inspection and approval scheme for manufactured hang gliders (there was by then an association of manufac-turers); and instituted a testing and licensing scheme that all pilots had to undergo before they could take part in national competitions. Later, they appointed officers concerned with safety, accident analysis and the inspection of hang gliding schools.

Though, as we indicated in the introduction, many enthusiasts resent this curbing of their freedom to fly when they like and where they like, it was the price that. it was necessary to pay in order to convince government departments, both local and national, that the sport was not an irresponsible one. That unfortunate image had been firmly planted on it by the time the BHGA's work began to bear fruit, and not altogether without reason. Had the BHGA not taken the action it did, the demands of some hysterical Members of Parliament to have the sport banned would almost certainly have found public support. Though the incidence of fatal hang-gliding accidents in Britain has never been high, there were too many not to disturb the conscience of the nation.

Of the local clubs in the country, the Southern Hang Gliding Club is the largest, serving Britain's most densely populated area. Unfortunately for the high concentration of fliers in south-east England, the prevailing winds are from the south and most of the suitable slopes face north, which leads inevitably to desperate overcrowding of sites on good days. When the south-westerly blows there are only seven locations in the whole of southern Britain suitable for hang gliding. One of them, Mill Hill in Sussex, became ·the subject of a protracted wrangle with the local authority and an appeal to the national Ministry. One of the objections to its use for hang gliding was that motorists on a nearby trunk road, from which there is an excellent view of the flying, were liable to become dangerously distracted from their business of high-speed motoring. If that is to be a consideration, the fliers pointed out, much else in life must be in danger of being banned—notably the female of the species.

More spectacular, though often less accessible, sites are available in many parts of the country. At the end of 1976, the BHGA had approximately 2,750 individual members and 32 member clubs. There were then 57 major clubs in Britain and another 30 of lesser stature, bringing to between four and five thousand the number of people in the country taking part in the sport. The BHGA only admits to full membership those clubs it considers large enough to sustain a strong committee (including a safety officer), and to publish a regular newspaper. Through this, the Association can ensure that they can communicate to all fliers—a vital matter if standards of safety and good practice are to be constantly improved.

Briton Richard Bickel leaves the White Cliffs of Dover behind in June 1975 as, on a 500 foot line, he starts the first kite trip across the English Channel. The journey to Calais took less than an hour.

It is probably the complaint of all the British clubs—and indeed of hang gliding throughout the world—that the sport attracts active idealists who want to get out and do it, and too few are prepared to lend a hand at the necessary organization and administration, chores which in this sport are more important than in most others. It is not just a matter of writing letters or keeping the cash. New models from the manufacturers must be inspected and tested, training schools must be kept under constant surveillance.

During that first busy year of its existence, the BHGA became a member of the Royal Aero Club, the controlling body for aviation sport in Britain, and attended an historic occasion in Paris. This was the inaugural meeting of the International Hang Gliding Commission, an arm of the ruling world aviation body, the Fédération Aéronautique Internationale. It was presided over by Ann Welch, the distinguished British aviator and glider pilot who had also chaired the meeting at which the BHGA was formed. The Paris conference provided the first opportunity for a detailed exchange of views and experience by hang-gliding administrators from all over the world and, more formally, began work on detailing international standards of all kinds. What will perhaps prove to be of greater importance eventually was that it gave the sport status and international respectability—even if those virtues are not always accorded to it domestically.

Many of the British problems of overcrowding and local authority intervention are also experienced in Australia, despite its vast size and small population. Hang gliding there is almost entirely concentrated in the coastal areas surrounding the five main cities, in which three-quarters of the nation's 13 million people live. It is a comparatively flat country, and most of the flying takes place from the eroded cliffs and large sand dunes of the beaches. The most popular sites are heavily overcrowded, and with a national growth rate that was running at about a hundred new fliers a month in 1976, that situation will only be resolved by greater determination in finding new sites. The flatness of the country, incidentally, led to the award of the Flat Land Trophy, a plaque given to pilots who maintain flight for not less than ten minutes, in a wind of not more than 15 mph, from a hill not higher than 35 feet. It was won almost as soon as the ink was dry on the conditions.

Australia has seven State hang gliding associations, and the paternal, co-ordinating, federal one of TASSA—The Australasian Self-Soar Association. (Soaring is no problem, in the strong and steady winds of those coasts, and that, rather than distance gliding, is the predominant occupation.) TASSA organizes and administers all matters that pertain directly to flying, and the State associations satisfy local requirements. TASSA seems to have an excellent working relationship with the Department of Transport, the Federal Government body responsible for aviation. Flying at one of the country's best sites, Stanwell, conflicted with jet aircraft coming into land at

French glider; bare-headed French pilot.

93

Sydney airport. Hang gliders were not banned: air traffic was re-routed, and hang gliders allocated positive air space—from half a mile inland to half a mile out to sea, rising to a height of 2,000 feet.

TASSA, which grew from a group of fliers in the Sydney area, operates a pilot rating scheme with seven levels of skill. Sites are similarly rated, and no pilot is allowed to fly from a site above his rating. State safety directors may vary the rating of a site according to the conditions of the day, and every site has a safety officer to whom pilots have to show their rating card. Fliers breaking these rules are liable to be fined. This elaborate and restrictive system has had spectacular success: though there are accidents, there has been, at the time we write, not one fatality in the history of Australian hang gliding.

There are contributory factors to this. Australians believe that prime among these is the fact that their gliders are, and always have been, well ahead of the field. Two of the great figures of hang gliding, Bennett and Moyes (whose achievements are discussed in the American chapter) came from tow-kiting in Sydney, and their craft were the models on which most Australian hang gliders were based.

Activity 'down under' is incessant. Left, Stanwell Park, Sydney; right, one of New Zealand's hot spots; below, Aussie team manager Bill Moyes with a Stinger; and Kev Cowie gets a good look at North Island from the height of Roturua's Mount Nyougotaha.

New South African endurance record being set by Eric Roberts, of the Albatross Club, in 1975. Floating over Sandy Bay, the 40 year old pilot stayed up one minute over six hours.

Hanging off Rhossili, Gower Peninsula, S. Wales.

Even in Rogallo designs, battens have always been used—four or five a side, parallel to the keel. That provides a ripple-free, flutter-free surface, which is not only more peaceful but, they contend, more efficient: slightly more lift, much less drag. Above all, the battens prevent sail collapse in high speed dives, severe stalls and excessive turbulence. The Australians claim— and it is difficult to argue against it—that this is the major contributing factor in their leading the world in the safety of the sport.

Though, as you look at hang gliding across the world, you find different techniques to cope with differing problems, the same human questions arise in every country where the popularity of the sport is great enough to impinge on the consciousness of the public: are we going to tolerate it, or do we reckon its intrusion is too aggravating to bear? What was the title of that short-lived American magazine?—*Low, Slow and Out of Control*. That is the point: you never know, the critics say, where the young devils are going to land. Since most of the flying in England, for example, is done over agricultural territory, the pilot does, from time to time, descend unwillingly on a farmer's crop or in a farmer's herd ('Fly like a bird, land in a turd' was suggested as the motto for the British Southern Hang Gliding Club). Hang gliding cannot get by without the co-operation of land owners, and national associations are constantly urging their members to heed all farmers' wishes—which do involve some sites closing completely during lambing, calving, harvesting and so on. Anything, everything, to maintain goodwill.

In other lands, other physical problems may predominate. In Australia, as you have seen, they can soar to their heart's content; in the mountainous far west of Canada, soaring is almost unknown. In Denmark, the only available take-off points are small coastal cliffs and an artificial hill formed from a rubbish tip. In Switzerland and Austria, it is all mountain and not much wind; in Hawaii, if you do not hang on tight, your glider will take off before you do. Ireland has the problem most others envy—more sites than hang gliders.

What are the worries of the hang-glider pilots of Andorra, Argentina, Belgium, Bolivia, Brazil, Chile, Costa Rica, Czechoslovakia, Finland, France, Germany, Greece, Haiti, Hungary, Israel, Italy, Japan, Kenya, Korea, Liechtenstein, Luxembourg, Mexico, Monaco, New Zealand, the Netherlands, Norway, Pakistan, Poland, Rhodesia, Romania, San Marino, South Africa, Spain, Sweden, Venezuela and Yugoslavia? Local problems they may have, big or small. You can be sure that, however successfully they deal with those, they will never solve the great, universal hang-gliding headache: why does the wind blow smooth and steady and from exactly the right quarter whenever it is your turn to stay at home and look after the baby?

David Cronk (USA) winning the 1974 international meet at Kossen, Austria.

On his first flight from the 9,750 foot peak of Austria's Ortler, Peter Nicklas of Innsbruck.

8 On Target

Competing is not in the nature of the average hang-glider enthusiast. His pleasure in his own achievements is immense, but only as measured against his own failures. If he is going to make a positive effort to gain height or distance, to manoeuvre precisely or to land accurately on a chosen spot, he would rather do it with the birds for the company than in front of a crowd. How many swimmers of your acquaintance, however effortless their style, enter races in the local pool? How many artists welcome eyes over their shoulder?

Nonetheless, the most skilful pilots, and those who acquire the most efficient of hang gliders, would be less than human if they were not keen to demonstrate their prowess, to make some notch on the official tally stick. Perhaps only half a dozen in a hundred care to do so, but at the rate hang gliding is spreading, even that number of potential competitors is considerable. Accordingly, the hang gliding calendar is dotted with regular regional, national and international meetings, and their organizers have always faced a mighty problem in the matter of how to measure ability in the fairest way, and in a way that is attractive to the spectator. For though, the sport being what it is, it may be difficult to make the public pay to see it, rich rewards can be reaped by making them pay to park their cars, particularly in advantageous positions. (The national organizations do need the money, much of which is spent in putting on better and safer meetings, so in a way the public get their money back.)

To satisfy these conditions, the competition needs to begin and end within public view; both its purpose and its method must be clear to the layman; and its execution should not only entertain him, but exercise the hang glider and its pilot as widely and as finely as possible within the bounds of personal and public safety. That is a framework that immediately restricts the possibilities, and they begin to narrow further when the organizer considers his first basic need: a site.

As he has clearly got to find and publicize the site at least six months before

Encamped as on a medieval battlefield, 300 contestants for the British Championships at Mere, Wiltshire, prepare for combat.

the event, he must choose one that will be flyable in the largest possible range of wind directions and speeds. A hill with a flying area that faces only one way, even if that is the way of the prevailing wind, will be disastrous if the competition period is one of those rare times when the wind blows the other way, or not at all, or too much. What if it is a great flying site, but has no public access? Or insufficient room for car parks, marquees, and the competitors' tents and caravans? Or, given all those facilities, just happens to be so situated that the recovery arrangements from landing spot back to take-off point are impossibly difficult?

Hang gliding provides problems for the competition organizer that no other sport has to contemplate, but let us presume he has overcome most of them. What is he going to ask the pilots to do—what is the spectator going to see? There will be no conventional racing, that is certain: two hang gliders flying on the same course at the same time is a recipe for disaster. It is possible that you could see a timed speed test of the same kind as a downhill ski run, one at a time against the clock, from the top of the hill to the bottom, either over a line or onto a target; simple to organize, simple to measure, but it is asking for trouble. There are enough traps for the wary flier in this sport, as we have seen, without encouraging the reckless one. What you are more likely to see are events that combine skill in the air—either at maintaining height or at manoeuvring round imaginary objects, or possibly both—with accuracy of landing.

Spot landing on its own is one of those events that is attractive to the organizer, by virtue of its simplicity, but soon palls for the spectator. Each flier takes off from the same point and aims for the same target, a 'bull's eye' down below. For maximum points, the flier must land with his feet on the centre spot—and that, for international events, is a ten-centimetre disc in the middle of a fifty-metre target. The flier must remain standing, and his glider must not touch the ground—otherwise it is known as a 'fall down' landing, which wins no points. (A splendid story from Ireland recalls the target being centred on a somewhat boggy spot; one flier, coming down much too fast, hit the spot but rapidly sank. He struggled to keep the machine from touching the ground, but lost in the end, by which time he was in it up to his waist.)

A spot landing competition can be arranged with the target at the end of a down-wind leg. The pilot must take off into the wind as usual, reach the area down wind, then turn for his landing into the wind again. Though this

Major competitions are a showcase for manufacturers, a chance to meet old friends, an excuse for a party, an excuse for another party, an opportunity to get up to date with developments and a time when leading fliers decide on tactics for the day.

Ready to go, one of the world's out-standing pilots, the late Bob Wills (USA). Ready to land, a pilot coming in spot on target.

exercises his skill and judgment more finely, it is more easily upset by wind change. In soaring conditions, the target can be located at the top of the hill instead of the bottom—a neat twist that you are not likely to find in major competitions, largely because it puts the public at risk.

Slalom courses test the pilot's accuracy in rounding fixed markers or passing through 'gates'. Though they are in fact only ground marks, they have to be thought of as pylons of infinite height. Every marker must have an observer,

An early 'flying plank', the British Breanwave, with a pilot supine and crowd agog.

whose job it is to judge whether the 'pylon' has been properly cleared by the pilot and his machine, and for the purpose the observer sometimes uses a sighting system in which mirrors give him perfect vertical vision. The pilot can win points either for the number of 'pylons' he can clear before he ceases to be airborne, or the number he clears in a given time, or the time he takes to complete a course.

In soaring conditions, this exercise can be developed into a more intriguing contest. Two 'pylons' are set as turning points at the top of the hill, and pilots are marked according to the number of times they can round them in a fixed time. To accomplish this, they increase speed, which loses them height. It soon becomes a fine test of pilot judgment, on how much of the one they can sacrifice in gaining the other. They then glide down, out of the lifting area, towards a landing area at the bottom. But before they reach it, there are other optional turning points affording more marks to those whose glide angle is good enough to leave them with sufficient height to round those, too. A word

about glide angle: that is the angle of the glide path to the horizontal, and the best is the flattest. A standard Rogallo hang glider has a glide ratio of about four to one, meaning that it should travel four metres across the ground for every one it drops in height.

Distance covered in a flight into wind is a simple task to undertake and to administer, though it may not intrigue the experienced pilot. It is an excellent exercise for the novice and pleasant entertainment for the spectator, who is treated to the sight of successful pilots triumphantly moving the marker flag along as they better the preceding distance.

A more skilful and complex exercise allows the pilot to gain distance in any direction, but this has the disadvantages of being extremely difficult to administer and not visually appealing to the spectator, who cannot judge progress when it is made in different directions.

Height gain from take-off point is fascinating to watch apart from the fact that, again, it is not possible for the spectator to judge competitive success. The height is usually recorded on a sealed barograph taken up by the pilot, but ideally should be measured by radar from the ground.

Duration of flight was a world championship competition at Kossen, Austria, in 1976. Despite its simplicity of measuring, it can be a terrible headache to the organizer. If soaring conditions unexpectedly develop, his schedule can be wrecked by flights of almost infinite duration.

Two more events deserve listing here, though there is no restriction on what might be devised by a cunning competition organizer. These are both high-calibre tests of pilot skill in all branches of gliding, though they contain unavoidable complexities that make them perhaps more potentially interesting than practically valuable. A *multiple option flight path* requires the pilot to proceed from take-off as quickly as possible to pass over a ground line just beyond the area of lifting wind. That done, he gains points by rounding various 'pylon' markers, each of which brings a score proportional to its distance away from the straight line between take-off and landing points. He may choose to go for big scores far away, or remain content to harvest as many of the near ones as he can. When the hang glider has lost so much height that he cannot attempt more, the pilot settles into the correct glide angle to bring him to the landing target.

A pilot competing in the World championships at Kossen, Austria, 1976. The spot landing bullseye is a 10 centimetre disc in the middle of a 50 metre target.

What about *cross-country* gliding? This would be a race against the clock over a long distance, with competitors starting at safe intervals. It would contain elements of orienteering and of cyclo-cross, for the pilot would have to decide the best route to take to attain the objective. He would have to find the path that gave him the best lift, the best speed, the best gliding; and since the route would no doubt cross a 'dead' area, such as a river valley, he would

be faced with landing, de-rigging and footing it over to the next possible take-off point. Clearly, there are monstrous difficulties involved in overseeing the operation, and possibly overwhelming ones in obtaining permission from all the land owners on the route to use their territory; but what a competition it might be!

Hang gliders come in all shapes and sizes: Kossen, 1976.

The first world championships, incidentally, were held at Kossen in March, 1975. The first approved by the newly formed Commission were at the same venue in September, 1976. The 1977 championships, due to be held in South Africa, were cancelled. They will from now on occur every two years. Leading candidates for 1979 and 1981 are, at the time we write, France and Great Britain.

There is another side to hang gliding competitiveness: the setting of individual records. In the nursery days of the sport, in whatever country it is growing up at the time, there are understandably proud efforts to stay up in the air longer than anyone else. In the United Kingdom, for instance, there was great excitement when, in November 1973, Len Gabriels soared aloft for 25 minutes 46 seconds (at the end of that time, he said: 'My fingers were really painful with the cold, and the pleasure had gone out of the flight'). Within a year, another of the country's leading fliers, Brian Wood, had reached 8 hours 26 minutes. During that time he was fed, air-to-air, with a crushed pasty and a can of beer that erupted when he opened it. At the end of the flight, he could not stand. When the International Hang Gliding

Commission first met the following summer, they agreed that sheer duration attempts would not be recognized as records. In most places, they are now actively discouraged. With the growing expertise of the pilots, and the increased performance of their machines, conditions can be found in which the only limit to time-in-the-air is that of physical exhaustion—at the time of Wood's effort from a 200 foot Welsh hill, the world 'record' stood at 10 hours 47 minutes, from a 2000 foot mountain in Hawaii. Nothing was to be gained, the administrators of the sport agreed, from tempting fliers to approach that dangerous barrier.

Straight distance is a record that is recognized, and that too soon reached incredible figures. The ever-active British pilot Ken Messenger took off from the summit of Mount Snowdon in September 1973 and covered three miles in a 15 minute flight. Less than three years later American Gene Blythe made a cross-country flight of 26 miles in Southern California after an altitude gain (another area in which records are approved) of 8,800 feet above take-off.

And so they go on, and will continue to go on. Some even go up attached to the baskets of hot-air balloons, to be released by the balloon pilot at astronomic heights. That too is now frowned on officially. It is, after all, ninety-nine per cent daredevil, and that is not the image hang gliding wants. Perhaps the records that are most important to the sport are those personal ones that bring smiles on the lowest slopes: 'Did you see that? I was up for a minute, a whole minute!'

Man will travel. Hang glider pilot at England's Mill Hill may cast a jaundiced eye on road-bound travellers, and go his own way, just like the birds.

9 Bicycles of the Air

Hang gliders will be commonplace by the year 2000. They will be the bicycles of the air. People who today regard the sport's enthusiasts as cranks will, twenty years from now, be accustomed to seeing them pass overhead, numbered among the rooks, competing with the gulls. The birds do have certain advantages, but then they had a few million years' start on the Rogallos. The hang-gliding fraternity are working on it. There are things they are learning about birds, especially those that soar, gaining height with ridiculous ease without a moment's effort. Look at the high aspect ratio wings of the gulls and the other sea-soaring birds—a long, long span, but very narrow. See too how the birds that soar over land, like the eagle, have split feathers at their wingtips. What is all that about? Is that an idea worth remembering?

Prophesying the future of hang gliding is dangerous, not so much because the prophet is likely to be wildly optimistic, but because in an area that develops as rapidly as this one, his dreams are likely to become realities before he can tell them. Today's new machine is outmoded in three months. Yesterday's record is tomorrow's standard—who would have believed just two years ago that anyone would hang-glide 107 miles in one flight? And even now, as you read this, what distances may already have been reached? We do know that designers are constantly striving for improved performance, and are fairly constantly succeeding. This means that year by year hang gliders are going to be manufactured with better glide angles and lower sink rates, gliders that will stay up longer and travel further. To achieve this, they will probably have to look less like Rogallos and more like folding gliders: they will have to copy the birds and use long, thin wings, whatever difficulties of handling this brings.

Allied with these improvements in performance will come a greater awareness of the need to find and use thermal lifts, those areas in which heated air rises from the ground like bubbles in liquid. (Thermal lifts are seldom visible, but are marked at the top of the 'chimney' by cumulus cloud.)

The high-aspect ratio of the wings of the sea-soaring birds has already influenced the high-performance designers. What can we learn from the split tips of those that soar over land?

By rising on a thermal, and having a sufficiently good glide angle to be able to reach the next one, much greater distances can be covered. Wave lifts too are relatively unexplored, and to operate satisfactorily in this area, both the pilot and his craft will have to be better prepared. Wave lifts, discussed earlier in this book, are great bands of rising air that flow over certain hill formations. They can present the pilot with embarrassing, and sometimes dangerous, altitude gains—to as much as 20,000 feet above the hill top.

To withstand the stress of such a lift, which can be disturbingly fast, the hang glider must be stronger. And if he is to reach anything like such heights, the pilot must be armed against the cold, which could be intense enough to freeze him to death, and the lack of oxygen, one of the first results of which is to destroy judgment. When he reached danger, the pilot would be unlikely to recognize it. Add to all that the fact that he may well find himself in cloud, and you will see that the hang glider will also have to be well supplied with instruments.

The changes we have so far discussed are totally predictable extensions of current hang gliding. One development at least awaits, which would be a revolution: power. Power in a glider? In a hang glider? Do we hear cries of 'Rubbish'? Now, wait: there are already those who have fitted motors on to hang gliders, and the potential is tremendous. There is no way that those who are keen are going to be prevented from working on this, so we ought to consider the possibilities.

If it were possible, when the pilot has reached the summit of his lift and the extent of the glide that follows it, for him to propel himself to the next area of lift, a new world of hang gliding would immediately be open. He could think of cross-country hang gliding over distances that at present he cannot contemplate, and those areas where at present the sky is sometimes too full of

Bicycles of the air? Bill Bennett rides here with an engine strapped to his back—a worrying device known in the business as a bum-chopper. This may not be the answer, but plenty of others are on the way for back-yard take-off.

the sport could be left to those who do not want to stray too far from base. If that can be done, and we know it can, then why not power-assisted take-offs? Nobody is going to recommend that you take-off from your back garden, unless it is bounded by fields; but once you were out of a built-up area, or could get to a beach, there is no reason why, like the birds, you should not rise to a safe height, find the lifting air, and start soaring. And then start travelling.

When you think of motorizing a hang glider, you come at once to problems. It needs a remarkably small engine—the sort you carry up ladders in a chain saw—but even that weighs about as much as the entire empty hang glider. The centre of gravity of the craft must not be disturbed, which means that this extra weight will have to be added just where the pilot hangs. An engine immediately above his head may not add to his delight; a propellor within reach certainly will not. Designers are now experimenting with centrally slung engines driving propellors elsewhere, and no doubt the answers are just round the corner.

This inevitable revolution is simply astounding in the possibilities it brings with it. The development could be as important to the world as that of the motor car was. Given the necessary technological advances and given public acceptance (and with it local authority co-operation), we are now talking about an instant, portable aeroplane. Not one that needs a team of ground staff, or a vast airfield with concrete runways, or huge quantities of high-priced fuel; one that you can keep in the garage and service yourself—or take along the road to your service station—and launch or land on a few square yards of grass.

A leading light in the fixed-wing brigade is the Easy Riser biplane, shown in action left, and, below, in a power-assisted version. Right is the high-performance Manta, with wing-tip steering and curved wing profile.

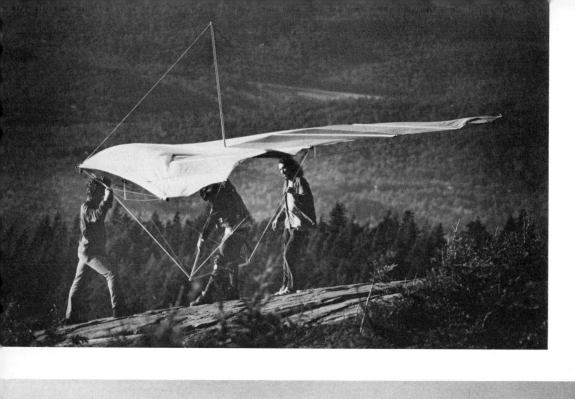

Above left, Kestrel and, below it, a Phoenix 8. Both trap air in the leading edge pocket to give an aerofoil cross-section when the kite flies. Above, a Miles Wing Gryphon that has no crosstube but a braced-wire leading edge.

As the suggestion becomes achievement, there will doubtless be a period of public hysteria. You may recall that the advent of the motor car was similarly received. It was allowed to travel at three miles an hour, as long as somebody walked ahead carrying a red flag. There will be those who view with horror what they predict as the overcrowding of the air, as if the craft will be jostling one another like twenty-two men on a football pitch. But there is an awful lot of space up there. Our space, ours to use. Mid-air collisions among aeroplanes are extremely rare, and almost always occur when the two craft are in a controlled zone, and being directed into or out of the same path. Think of the air over London and south-east England during the summer of 1940; hundreds of planes with tired pilots, all uncontrolled from the ground and doing their best to get into each other's way. Many died, but very, very few as the result of collisions. And is it not surprising, on the roads, how quickly we became used to hurtling within a metre or two of scores of other cars, each weighing about a ton, passing each other at a combined speed of 100 mph? We moan about overcrowded roads, too, but mostly because the car in front prevents us from going any faster.

The advent of power-assistance is bound to split the sport of hang gliding. There will always be room for the purist, for the man who wants to be like a bird and rates the thought of an internal combustion engine on his wings as a very nasty one indeed. Within the sport, there will always be a class for him; and probably one for the man who uses thrust to maintain height, and one for the man who also uses thrust for take-off. Those whose hang gliders become portable aircraft will be subjected to the regulations and licences of their aviation authorities, but the likelihood has already been established, at least in the United Kingdom, that hang gliders using power merely as an extension of a sporting and recreational activity will remain under the control of their own association.

Lest you think that we have wandered into science fiction in this chapter, we should remind you that an American aeronautical engineering firm,

Ryans, devised a powered craft based on a Rogallo wing at least ten years ago. It was capable of carrying a load of one and a half tons and was known as the Fleep. The commercial potential of such a machine is extensive, particularly in agricultural work, and particularly in those countries where the cost of maintaining regular aircraft for such irregular jobs is prohibitive; but it is when you contemplate a hang glider's military possibilities that the eyes begin to open really wide.

Apart from the simple capability of unpowered Rogallos to carry a platoon of infantrymen silently down an impossible hill in a guerilla-style operation, imagine what destruction could be let loose by powered hang gliders that were radio-controlled and used to carry missiles. Remember the V-I weapon used by Germany in the Second World War? A pilotless flying machine with a twenty-foot wing span and a relatively low aspect ratio. The engine was incredibly crude and simple, but enough to carry a ton of explosives from northern France to London. A similar propulsion system for a Rogallo-type wing would create a 40 mph guided missile aircraft that would not register on most radar screens and could cost less than £100. At that price, they could be launched by the hundred. They could be carried in Land Rovers and launched anywhere by three or four men, and it hardly bears thinking about; but there is hardly a reason why it could not happen.

Have they done it all now? Left : manufacturers test new machines at the Steyning Bowl, England. None of them goes as far away from the initial Lilienthal/Rogallo concept as this Mitchell Wing, below, probably the most advanced hang glider in the world. As it comes in to land, air brakes are on and the pilot is partly concealed in a windowed cockpit. Put an engine on that and where are you? Not flying like a bird, that's for sure. More like an, um . . . aeroplane? In 1977 George Worthington flew an unpowered Mitchell Wing a straight distance of 107.8 miles.

Most developments have the potential of being used for good or for evil, and hang gliders are no exception. They do have an evil application, but everybody in the sport would be much happier to see them used for good. The possibilities are many, and intriguing. Some have already, spontaneously, been tested. After the rape of a girl in deserted Australian countryside, hang glider pilots joined the search for her attacker. Long before police on foot were able to reach the area, gliders were criss-crossing the air space from their perfect vantage points.

At Rhossili, best-known hang-gliding site in South Wales, somebody fell over the cliff edge and was trapped on its face, out of sight from above. The only way to locate the casualty seemed to be to get the coastguards to launch a boat and search the cliff from the sea—until a hang-glider pilot volunteered to take off from the cliff top and guide rescuers to the right spot.

It is interesting, incidentally, to note one of the alternative applications of hang gliding technology that has become internationally popular: the recognition of the fact, by Squadron-Leader Dunsford and Peter Powell, that by adding an extra string to an ordinary toy kite it was possible to produce one that not only flew almost infallibly, but was manoeuvrable, under the control of the operator on the ground. Apart from leading to millions of them flying from the beaches and commons of the world, the idea

has already proved invaluable for remote-controlled aerial photography for survey and archaeological work. The principle could well be developed in other directions—as a method for transporting power lines across inaccessible gaps, for instance, for breeches buoy rescue, for crop seeding.

As aeroplanes and rockets advance further, and burn up more and more of the world's rapidly-decreasing fuel supplies (which could soon become so dear that we could not afford to use them), it looks as though aeronautical development can go no further forward. Where it can fruitfully and joyfully go is backwards. Back to riding on air. Just like the birds.

Code of Good Practice

This is the Code of Good Practice required of its members by the British Hang Gliding Association. Similar standards are, or should be, set all over the world. Several of its clauses apply as much to spectators as to fliers.

1 **a** Ensure that the permission of the land owner, occupier or controlling authority has been obtained before using a site.
b When seeking permission to fly, always present your BHGA and Club membership cards.
c State exactly where you wish to fly and where you intend to land.
d When visiting sites administered by other clubs, always contact them in advance and observe their local rules.
e Do not fly from a site when livestock are about to bear their young (lambing, calving and having foals). This is usually the late March–May period and varies with breed and locality. Check with the farmer.

2 **a** If your flying activities are likely to cause traffic congestion, inform the local police.
b All soaring sites should be known to the Military Air Traffic Organization. Pilots of low-flying aircraft are briefed to avoid these areas. Please report any new soaring site to the Secretary of the BHGA so that MATO can be informed.
c Drive considerately—you are easily identifiable with your glider on the roof.
d Park your car with due consideration for others, especially when loading or unloading. Find a proper parking space (not the grass verge). The admission of vehicles to club flying sites should be discouraged.